The Nonsuch

The Nonsuch

A. Small

by
Laird Rankin

CLARKE, IRWIN & COMPANY LIMITED/TORONTO, VANCOUVER

© 1974 by Clarke, Irwin & Company Limited

ISBN 0 7720 0731 4

Published simultaneously in the United States
by Books Canada, Inc., 33 East Tupper Street,
Buffalo, N.Y. 14203, and in the United Kingdom
by Books Canada Limited, 17 Cockspur Street,
Suite 600, London SW1Y 5BP

1 2 3 4 5 6 BP 79 78 77 76 75 74

Printed in Canada

To Adrian Small, for his days on the Nonsuch;
to Scott Rankin, for his future

Acknowledgments

I am indebted to the Hudson's Bay Company for access to and use of Company material and photographs, and for permission to quote from its Archives.

My thanks to the following people for allowing me to quote from their letters: The Right Honourable Viscount Amory, K.D., P.C., G.C.M.G., T.D., D.L., London, England; Mr. A. R. Huband, Winnipeg; Mr. L. A. Learmonth, Georgetown, Ontario; Mr. J. Richard Murray, Ottawa; Captain A. F. Raynaud, Seattle, Washington; Captain Adrian Small, Brixham, England; Mr. Alfred Weatherill, Brixham; Mr. J. L. Williams, Seattle; and Mr. Peter M. Wood, London, England.

My thanks also to the *Ladysmith-Chemainus Chronicle,* Ladysmith, British Columbia, for permission to quote from an editorial.

I am grateful to the following for permission to reproduce photographs for use in this book:

CP Picture Service, p. 19

Denis Cahill, *The St. Catharines Standard,* p. 65

Central Studios Photography, Exeter, England, p. 43

Bill Cunningham, pp. 98, 101

Hudson's Bay Company, for the following photographs from its collection: photo by Bristol City Line Ltd., p. 48; photo by Gunnar Photography, p. 105; photos by A. R. Huband, pp. 49, 67, 119; photos by A. C. Littlejohns, Bideford, England, pp. 10, 11, 20, 22, 23, 25, 32, 37; photo by Bob Murphy, p. 74; photos by W. R. Pearce, pp. 70, 84, 85 (right), 88, 89, 102, 109; photos by Adrian Small, pp. 85 (left), 103

Keystone Press Agency, London, England, p. 39

The Guardian, Manchester, England, p. 29

Manitoba Museum of Man and Nature, pp. 118, 120

The News, Portsmouth, England, p. 24

The Niagara Falls Review, p. 63

Nigel Racine, p. 40

The Vancouver Sun, pp. 96, 99

In addition I wish to thank the National Postal Museum for permission to reproduce the *Nonsuch* stamp on page 8, and the Hudson's Bay Company for use of the illustrations on pages *iii,* 4, 7, 16, 21, 34, 47, 55, 59, 62, 78, 107, and 128.

Particular thanks are due to Adrian Small, who has permitted use of his fine drawings on pages 46, 56, 94, and 125.

The day I went aboard the *Nonsuch* for the first time, she was bobbing gently on the Thames, alongside a pier in Greenwich, England. I sat in the Great Cabin at the stern of the ship while Captain Small expounded the features of his vessel, but I heard little of what he said; I was longing to return to shore and calm the tempest that was brewing in my stomach. So began a four-year association with the *Nonsuch*. Mercifully, I soon acquired my sea legs.

The Hudson's Bay Company had hired me in late 1967 to plan and publicize the travels of the *Nonsuch* when she came to Canada in 1970. During the three seasons I arranged her tours, she proved a promoter's delight. But while it was simple enough to make the public aware of the *Nonsuch,* the presence of a seventeenth-century ketch amid twentieth-century conditions created some challenging logistical problems. To me, however, she became more than a public relations assignment; it was impossible not to fall under her spell. The sight of the *Nonsuch* under sail, with canvas stretched and flags flying, quickly erased all memory of the difficulties she had caused, and each time I watched her arrive in port and witnessed the joy she gave so effortlessly to those on shore, my emotional attachment to her grew stronger.

The men of the *Nonsuch* crew, her remarkable captain, Adrian Small, and the late Commander Peter Winter all contributed to the success of the *Nonsuch* venture, and there were hundreds more, in the United Kingdom and in Canada, who gave generously of their time to help arrange the ship's tour. Sadly, they remain unsung heroes, for a list of those who befriended the *Nonsuch* would probably exceed the length of this book.

I am not a man of the sea; in fact the *Nonsuch* is the only ship I have known. Some readers may be disappointed that there is not more of the sailor's viewpoint in the following pages, but my approach to this book was to present a factual account – and in part a personal view – of highlights in the life of an extraordinary ship, from the time when she was merely a wild idea until she was moored permanently in Winnipeg for future generations to see.

Winnipeg, 1974   LAIRD RANKIN

Contents

Note: In this book, mileage is stated in nautical miles (6,080 feet) unless otherwise indicated.

The Nonsuch

The seventeenth century – an age of sail, of drama on the seas. In
Europe it was an expansive era of remarkable international accom-
plishment, when only elementary aids and unsophisticated equipment
were available to transport a pioneering spirit to a far-off land. It
was a time when men of rugged courage were drawn to the New
World by dreams of discovering the North-West Passage to the
Orient with its rich markets. Success eluded them, but the results
of their exploits were far from negligible: new waters were charted;
new lands were explored; resources, particularly fur, were discovered; and the seeds of settlement and trade in North America
were sown.

Jacques Cartier had discovered the St. Lawrence River in 1534,
and less than one hundred years later, Samuel de Champlain had
founded a colony on its north shore. By the middle of the seventeenth century, French settlement along the river was well established and a profitable fur trade empire had developed, with
perimeters that extended beyond the river to include the Great
Lakes region to the west. The forests north of the Lakes were the
source of many of the skins brought to the French villages. These
wooded lands had everything desired by the beaver – ample streams
and lakes, and an abundance of aspen, poplar, willow and birch, his
favourite foods. The Cree Indians of the region trapped the beaver
and other fur-bearing animals and traded the pelts to tribes who
transported them by canoe over an indirect route of rivers and lakes
to the depots on the St. Lawrence. Ships carried the furs to France
where they were made into handsome felt hats, the current fashion
in Europe. The French-Canadian fur trade system was complicated,
but it was thriving and it held a monopoly position. There was no
need to streamline.

At some point in the 1650's – there is uncertainty about the
exact date – two French fur-traders embarked on a journey which
eventually revolutionized the fur trade. Médard Chouart, Sieur des
Groseilliers, and his brother-in-law, Pierre Esprit Radisson, travelled
inland in North America, possibly as far as James Bay, trading and

Prologue

The First
Nonsuch

1

living with a number of Indian tribes, and studying the mechanics of the fur trade. When they returned from their travels, they were convinced that there was a more efficient way to tap the fur-rich forests of the North.

Radisson and Groseilliers were an adventurous pair of promoters whose combined talents and experience made them authorities on the fur trade of their time. They had forceful personalities and remarkable tales to tell, and they spoke of their ideas with enthusiasm and conviction. On the basis of their inland explorations, they proposed trading directly with the Cree, eliminating the middlemen, and using depots on Hudson Bay for loading the furs onto ships bound for England. The scheme offered the advantages of proximity to the current source of prime fur and a simplified system of trade. If proved practicable, however, it could shift the focus of the fur trade from the St. Lawrence to Hudson Bay, and threaten the revenues of the French colony. For this reason the two Frenchmen found no support for their proposals in either New or Old France.

Disappointed but not discouraged, the pair took their ideas to New England. In Boston they were successful in chartering a vessel, but the expedition failed to reach Hudson Bay. The Boston visit, however, introduced them to Colonel George Cartwright, an English commissioner in the Colonies, who was attempting to renew colonial loyalty to the Crown. Impressed with their stories, Cartwright brought the Frenchmen to England in 1665 and arranged a meeting with Sir George Carteret. Radisson and Groseilliers won the support of this influential courtier, and through him gained an audience with King Charles II, who expressed interest in their ideas and asked for a written account of their proposals.

It is easy to understand how these two engaging foreigners proposing a trading expedition into a faraway wilderness found a receptive audience at the court of King Charles. Although worldly and notoriously dissolute, charred by the Great Fire and weakened by the Plague, Restoration London persistently demonstrated a vigorous interest in the arts and sciences. There was a passion to conquer new fields, to transform the young Empire into a close fabric of commerce, colonies and sea power. Exploration and trade expressed the spirit of the time.

Through the King, Radisson and Groseilliers became acquainted with his cousin, Prince Rupert, and a circle of courtiers, financiers, scientists, and merchants, who quickly grasped the trade prospects of the Hudson Bay route. In 1667, Rupert and his associates acquired their first ship, the *Discovery,* but she was fitted out "to noe purpose," according to Radisson, and subsequently sold. On March 30 of the following year, these men paid £290 for another ship, a small square-rigged ketch called the *Nonsuch.*

On June 3, 1668, the *Nonsuch* weighed anchor at Gravesend. She was commanded by Zachariah Gillam, a seaman from Boston, and Groseilliers was on board. Radisson was on the *Eaglet,* loaned from the Royal Navy by the King, but she was forced back to England because of damage suffered in a storm off the Irish Coast and never completed the voyage.

No log of the Atlantic crossing has survived, but investigation of other sources has produced some illuminating data. Both captains received a set of elaborate instructions regarding discovery, settlement, minerals and especially fur. They were asked to keep journals, to prepare maps, and to be cautious when trading with the Indians. They were firmly ordered to sail "to such place as Mr Gooseberry and Mr Raddisson shall direct . . . in ordr to trade with the Indyans there," and to treat their important passengers "with all manner of Civility and Courtesy." To discourage trading for personal benefit, the financiers included a clause declaring "that if by accident you meet with any Sea Horse or Mors teeth or make any advantage by Killing of Whales It is to be made good to our accompt."

On board the *Nonsuch* was a diverse cargo of tar, compasses, medicines, axes, saws, hammers, blunderbusses, muskets, pistols, powder, shot, paper, quills and eel nets. There was salt pork and beef, and such luxuries as raisins, prunes, sugar, spice, lemon juice,

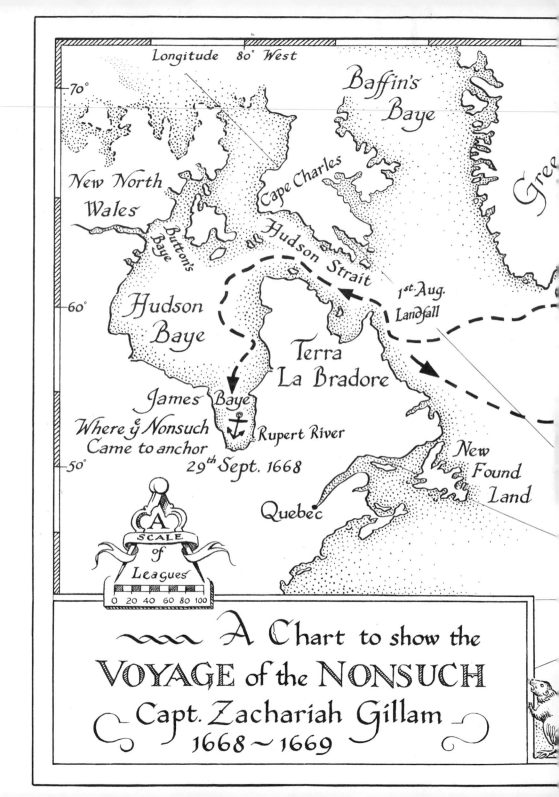

Longitude 80° West

—70°

Baffin's
Baye

New North
Wales

Cape Charles

Gree

Button's
Baye

—60°

Hudson
Baye

Hudson Strait

1st. Aug.
Landfall

Terra
La Bradore

James Baye

Where ÿ Nonsuch
Came to anchor
29th Sept. 1668

Rupert River

New
Found
Land

—50°

Quebec

A
SCALE
of
Leagues

0 20 40 60 80 100

A Chart to show the
VOYAGE of the NONSUCH
Capt. Zachariah Gillam
1668 ~ 1669

beer and brandy. There was also a supply of "wampumpeage," small shell beads which were the standard currency of the early fur trade and widely used as a medium of exchange. The best beads came from Long Island, New York, and Groseilliers had brought a supply with him to England for such a purpose as the expedition to Hudson Bay.

Besides entries for Captain Gillam and Groseilliers, the Hudson's Bay Company's first Grand Ledger shows three other accounts under the names of men who received wages for their services on the vessel: Thomas Shepard, chief mate, James Tatnam, mate, and Pierre Romieux, a French surgeon. The *Nonsuch* could probably have been handled comfortably by seven or eight men. One source claims that the complement of the *Nonsuch* in her Navy days was a dozen men in peace, two dozen in war abroad and thirty-five men in war at home.

From the Thames the *Nonsuch* sailed by a northerly route, following the east coast of England past the Orkney Islands to the Atlantic. On August 1, the north coast of Labrador was sighted, and four days later she was off Resolution Island at the entrance to Hudson Strait.

On September 29, 118 days after leaving Gravesend, the *Nonsuch* reached the south end of James Bay and anchored off the mouth of a river (in present-day Quebec) which the men named Rupert. The provisions were carried ashore and the crew set about building a house. Before snow covered the low-lying shores, they had completed Charles Fort, named in honour of the King. The fort, built of upright logs caulked with moss, with a twelve-foot cellar and a thatched roof, offered them little more comfort than the cramped ketch in the bay. It was their home over the long chilling winter.

With the welcome return of warm weather, the peaceful Cree Indians began to come to the Bay to trade. In his journal Captain Gillam stated that they traded with some three hundred of them. By June, with a cargo of prime beaver on board, the *Nonsuch* was ready for the return crossing, but because of ice in Hudson Bay, the departure was delayed until August.

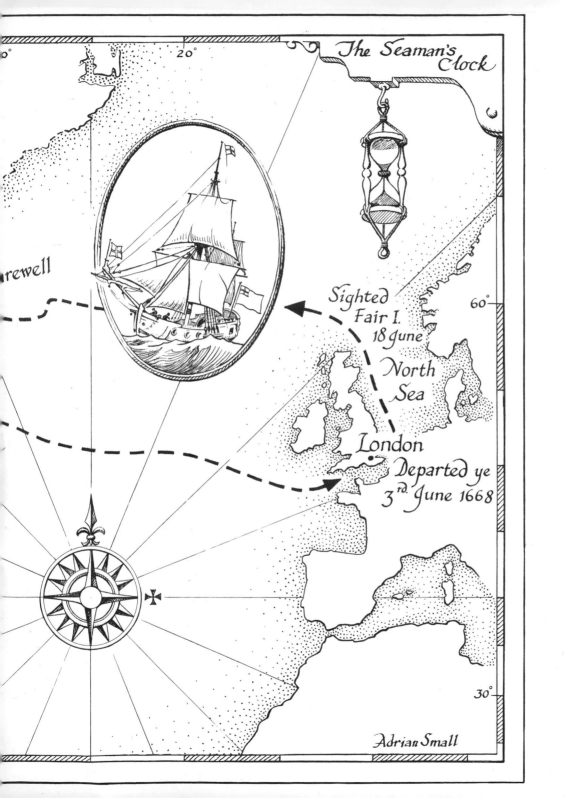

The Seaman's Clock

20°

60°

30°

Sighted
Fair I.
18 June

North
Sea

London

Departed ye
3rd June 1668

rewell

Adrian Small

**The first page of the royal charter founding
the Hudson's Bay Company, 2nd May, 1670**

On October 11, 1669, the *London Gazette* reported from Deal on Dover Strait: "This last night came in here the 'Nonsuch Ketch', which having endeavoured to make out a passage by the North-West, was in those seas environed with Ice, which opposing her progress, the men were forced to hale her on shoar and to provide against the ensueing cold of a long Winter; which ending they returned with a considerable quantity of Beaver, which made them some recompence for their cold confinement."

The cargo of beaver sold briskly and the ship fetched £152 10s. from a Captain Chappell in June, 1670, considerably less than the purchase price. While it is impossible to prepare a precise or meaningful balance sheet for the *Nonsuch* expedition, it is known that the sale of the ship and her cargo brought a sum insufficient to cover the expense of the crossing or the investment preceeding it. But the monetary loss was unimportant. The radical fur trade theory had been tried and proved; a ship's crew had survived a winter on Hudson Bay and brought back a cargo of furs which had sold readily on the London market. Bolstered by the evidence and encouraged by the prospects, the eighteen investors approached King Charles for a charter to trade. It was granted on 2nd May, 1670, founding the "Governor and Company of Adventurers of England trading into Hudson's Bay," commonly called by its compact title, the Hudson's Bay Company.

The Canadian stamp issued June 5, 1968, to commemorate the 300th anniversary of the departure of the *Nonsuch* for Hudson Bay

It was almost sunset on August 26, 1968. An opening-night air of excitement gripped the crowd that pressed to the water's edge. On the official reviewing platform, dignitaries shuffled notes and peered out over the expectant multitude. The tiny shipbuilding town had been swollen by nearly 38,000 visitors; the riverbank in the vicinity of the boat-shed was thick with people. Many of them, modestly demonstrating that peculiar British precaution against missing something special, had kept a vigil for three to four hours. To gain a better vantage point, several spectators waded into the water which was now reaching high tide. The crowd passed the time by listening to the ship's captain struggle through an incomplete speech or watching the various water craft as they vied for a view and prepared to greet the arrival of a sister with blasts of boat whistles, sirens and fireworks. Television, newspaper and film cameramen were there to record the event.

At eight o'clock the tide was in – the moment had come. A frail, elderly lady on the rostrum stepped forward, and mustering all her matronly muscle, swung the traditional bottle of champagne toward the ship's bow. On the third cast it obliged, and shattered. But the ship did not move. The officials on the platform stood by helplessly for what one of them described as "ten awful minutes"; the throng watched patiently, fascinated by the desperate chorus of hammering from the frantic shipyard staff who pushed, prodded and heaved. Still the ship would not move.

Then one old hand offered a seasoned thought: perhaps the grease under the vessel was acting as an adhesive, not as a lubricant. Why not jack up the bow slightly to send her sliding? It worked. She began to move at once and slipped smoothly, swiftly into the water – clipping a passing powerboat in her path – to the salute of her five cannons (the sixth misfired), shouts of joy, a salvo of honour and deafening cheers of welcome from the multitude.

For this was no ordinary vessel: she was a living vision of the bygone era of the square-rigger, and for many she tugged at the heart. She was a replica of the ketch *Nonsuch*. The sunset ceremony at Appledore, Devon, ended the vessel's long gestation period

Construction of the Replica

Mrs. L. Heathcoat Amory christens the *Nonsuch* in the company of Lord Amory, Mr. A. L. Hinks and Mr. R. Warington Smyth

The hull of the replica enters the water for the first time

which, like the launching, had offered its share of surprises, drama, comedy and success.

In late 1963, the Hudson's Bay Company in Winnipeg had begun collecting suggestions for appropriate ways to mark two forthcoming milestones: Canada's 100th anniversary of Confederation in 1967, and, three years later, the Company's tercentennial. Because the history of the Company was closely entwined with that

Part of the crowd of 38,000 at the launching ceremony in Appledore

of the nation, Company executives took it for granted that the Company would honour the Canadian anniversary in some way.

The approaching anniversaries gave rise to several suggestions to have the *Nonsuch* fully reconstructed. It was not an original idea for it had been suggested before by others both inside and outside the organization, but it had been treated lightly as the Company management considered it impractical and far-fetched. They could see no use for a maritime project to a company whose operations were predominantly inland. The chief objections, though, were the cost – an unknown that was assumed to be a fortune – and the absence of a final resting place for the vessel once she had ceased operation. By early 1964 the idea had been discarded.

Visiting Winnipeg in April 1966 was Mr. Melbourne Smith. Mr. Smith was a former sailing master, an accomplished marine artist and part-owner of a shipbuilding concern in British Honduras. He had been invited to the Company's Winnipeg office to explore the possibility of producing a series of paintings of Hudson's Bay Company sailing ships. The subject of the *Nonsuch* was raised, as it was logical, if not obligatory, to include a painting of the Company's first ship in the collection. Mr. Smith took the subject a step further. He looked at what material the Company had on the original *Nonsuch,* made some calculations, and estimated that a replica could be built for a maximum of $100,000. This was the first informed opinion the Company had received on the feasibility and cost of the undertaking. They were surprised by the modest estimate, but although it appeared that the *Nonsuch* could be recreated for a modest amount, something was still missing: they could see no end use for the ship.

A few days later the Company was approached by the Manitoba Centennial Corporation for a substantial contribution to a provincial centennial project: a cultural complex in downtown Winnipeg consisting of a concert hall, a planetarium and a museum. Company officials were agreeable, but instead of taking the conventional approach by simply writing a cheque, they considered a twist to the gift. The Company contribution, they felt, would be "more effective . . . if it could at least partly be paid in kind rather than cash, provided . . . something striking, unique and appropriate to H B C " could be conceived.

The almost simultaneous occurrence of these two independent developments was purely fortuitous; the timing was uncanny. Melbourne Smith had resurrected the *Nonsuch* idea just days before the centennial canvassers arrived on the Company doorstep. The provincial proposal for a museum was the link that had been missing before: a museum would happily integrate a salute to the nation's anniversary and a permanent home for the replica whose predecessor had opened a new chapter in Canadian history. The Centennial Corporation people were intrigued by the idea. With the two major impediments to the project reduced to realistic proportions, active pursuit of the idea began.

The Winnipeg office of the Company, however, could not develop the *Nonsuch* independently, for it was only one administrative half of a schizophrenic organization. The Hudson's Bay Company had been based in London, England, since its incorporation in 1670. It was there that the Board of Directors met regularly, and the Company's governor, or chairman of the Board, had traditionally been an Englishman. Nevertheless, the Company's vast commercial empire was almost entirely Canadian. In 1912, the administration of Canadian operations had been transferred to Winnipeg, to a group of men which became the Canadian Committee of the Board in 1922, and a managing director, also a Canadian, had been added in 1946. Hudson's Bay House in Winnipeg served as the Canadian headquarters until May 1970, when it was elevated to the Company's official head office, and in that same year the Company appointed its first Canadian governor. But until the headquarters came to Canada, decisions still ultimately rested with the Board of Directors thousands of miles away in London. It was a cumbersome administrative system and it fostered a comic tug-of-war for control of the *Nonsuch* project.

In May 1966 Winnipeg informed London of its proposal to build the ship as part of the Company's Centennial and 300th Anniversary programs, to operate her for two seasons in eastern Canada, and finally to bring her to Thunder Bay and then overland to Winnipeg where she would be presented to the Manitoba Museum. On the eighteenth of the month, the Board gave its enthusiastic support to an investigation of the proposal in order to determine the cost of construction.

Before construction estimates could be obtained, someone had to be selected to research the vessel and prepare a detailed set of plans and specifications. Winnipeg acknowledged that the work could best be done in England where the original ship had been built and where information on ketches of the period was more readily available. Winnipeg did not think, however, that the designer had to be a resident of the U.K. It expressed some "moral obligation to seriously consider Mr. Smith," for obvious reasons, provided he was "technically competent" to perform the task. London did not intervene, but while Winnipeg wrote to Mr. Smith's references, London conducted its own talent hunt.

Melbourne Smith's references spoke highly of him as a marine artist and a person skilled in marine historical research, but they could not comment on his ability as a naval architect. Mr. Smith outlined to the Company how he would work with such a person. Winnipeg's sense of obligation to Mr. Smith must have been strong, for although he was an artist, not a naval architect, and therefore technically unqualified for the post, Winnipeg refused to withdraw his name. Mr. J.R. Murray, the Canadian managing director, encouraged the Governor, Lord Amory, to interview Mr. Smith. The Governor was not persuaded.

Two names had been submitted to the Company in London. Each man was an associate member of the Royal Institution of Naval Architects and came with excellent recommendations from respected sources. Further information from the National Maritime Museum in Greenwich, England, indicated that of the two British candidates Mr. Rodney Warington Smyth was the most suitable to carry out the research and design the replica. Anxious for an immediate start, the Governor cabled Mr. Murray for his agreement to the appointment of Mr. Warington Smyth. Winnipeg shared London's eagerness to commence work, and realizing that it was engaged in a Quixotic battle with headquarters, and that its candidate was outranked by London's selection, Winnipeg acquiesced. Mr. Murray rubber-stamped the recommendation; Winnipeg's influence and control of the *Nonsuch* project was instantly diminished.

Mr. Warington Smyth was managing director of the Falmouth Boat Construction Company in Falmouth, Cornwall. Apart from his usual work designing and constructing small craft and yachts, he had had some experience designing replicas, and for the *Nonsuch* project he had the assistance of two men considered well versed in the subject of square-rigged sailing ships, Mr. Percy Dalton and Mr. Peter M. Wood.

Mr. Warington Smyth was appointed to the *Nonsuch* project in July 1966; he estimated completion of the drawings by mid-December. In this unique assignment, the design team faced two hurdles: lack of information about the original ketch and constructive suggestions from the Company's Canadian headquarters.

A ketch, by seventeenth-century definition, meant "a vessel with a tall mainmast in front and a small mizzen behind, setting square sails from both." It was a small ship typical of the deep-sea merchant ships of the period and 150 years thereafter.

The original *Nonsuch* had been acquired from a Sir William Warren who did considerable business with the Navy. It is likely that she was the ship of the same name sold by the Navy in 1667. If this assumption is correct, then she was built in Wivenhoe, Essex, in 1650 by a Mr. Page, bought by the Navy in 1654, captured by the Dutch in 1658, recaptured a year later and listed again as a naval ship in 1660. Navy records reveal that she was 36 or 37 feet on the keel, 15 to 15½ feet wide and had a burden, or cargo capacity, of between 43 and 47 tons. Peter Wood said, "In spite of having to write and answer hundreds of letters, we gained virtually no authentic gen on the *Nonsuch* except her dimensions."

15

The rest of the *Nonsuch* was a puzzle, and the balance of the replica was pieced together from exhaustive, skilled research into all aspects of ketches of the period, from materials to finishes. The team consulted several institutions, books and early manuscripts as well as the Archives of the Hudson's Bay Company. Reference drawings were made from seventeenth-century models and paintings. The team drew information from near-contemporary accounts of ship-building found in the National Maritime Museum, where they were assisted by George Naish, the Keeper of the Museum, an expert on the history of shipbuilding.

Winnipeg, undaunted by the defeat over Smith, forwarded *its* ideas for the *Nonsuch* design to London. The opinions were mainly

The return of the *Nonsuch* to London, October 1669; painted by Norman Wilkinson C.B.E. for the Hudson's Bay Company

those of a man whose nautical knowledge was unrivalled by anyone in the Company's Winnipeg offices, Captain F. M. Shaw, who was manager of the Transport Division of the Company's Northern Stores Department.

Captain Shaw had fresh views on the ship. He realized that the replica would have to conform to standards and demands unknown by the original, and he recommended that she be equipped with a small battery-charging generator for lights below deck and for navigation. He was aware of Winnipeg's intention to exhibit the ship in a variety of ports and he was convinced that if the Company relied on the elements to deliver the ship from place to place, a tour time-table would be an academic exercise, as uncertain as the weather itself. He urged that the *Nonsuch* be equipped with an auxiliary engine of medium speed, and suggested that 100 h.p. would be adequate.

To purists, these were bothersome, offensive proposals. London expressed delicately-phrased opposition to installing an engine, speculating that a motor bolted on the stern of the ship (hardly what Captain Shaw had in mind!) would upset her balance, quite apart from looking unsightly. Mr. Warington Smyth's alternative was to equip her with a tender, presumably to tow her on to the next stop. Captain Shaw expressed uncertainty that such an accessory would have sufficient power to propel the *Nonsuch* through stiff currents on the St. Lawrence River. London also objected to the matter of electric running lights: they would be out of character. Mr. Warington Smyth proposed that night passages be avoided to eliminate the need for lights.

(These international disagreements would eventually be settled peacefully. Neither side lost. Running lights *would* be added; nevertheless, the *Nonsuch* would also use oil navigation lamps and candle lamps in the Captain's quarters. The replica *would* be equipped with a 90 h.p. Perkins diesel engine, but she would have a tender as well, and subsequently a 22-foot shallop was built for the purpose.)

Winnipeg had always hoped to have the vessel constructed on the North American side of the Atlantic, and there was a rationale supporting this: she would be on the same side of the Atlantic as her future home and no transatlantic transportation costs would be involved. Melbourne Smith's firm, Simeon Young and Co., was a possible location, and Captain Shaw submitted a list of several capable Nova Scotia yards. The Company even approached the Atlantic Provinces Pavilion at Expo 67, which was to feature wooden shipbuilding, to inquire whether or not the Pavilion would like to undertake the *Nonsuch* project.

When the plans and specifications had been completed, the Company prepared to call for tenders to construct the ship. Captain Shaw was of the opinion that when this was done, some flexibility should be allowed for substituting native wood. London, however, argued pedantically in favour of traditional, bone-hard English oak. Mr. Warington Smyth was of the opinion that the oak left in England would be of much the same quality as the timber from which the *Nonsuch* had been built; furthermore, he thought that it was the best timber for natural bends and that it would be the right colour when varnished. Any other timber would alter the ship's weight, and require more ballast. An alternative to oak was unthinkable; a change from the basic material of the original would create an imposter, not a replica.

The choice of wood was unnegotiable; construction of the vessel in England was almost guaranteed. Of course, the timber could be brought to Canada, but in the estimate of one Canadian shipbuilding expert, this would increase the cost of the ship by 150 per cent. The future of Winnipeg's involvement in the *Nonsuch* was threatened; it was on the verge of becoming a silent partner.

London extended Winnipeg the courtesy of asking Canadian firms to tender if it thought there were any yards in Canada that should be given the opportunity. It was a corporate formality, a straw which Winnipeg chose to grasp as there were Canadian firms qualified for the job. London asked for tenders from seven firms. Winnipeg approached Smith and Rhuland (who built the *Bounty* and

Alan Hinks inspects the ship's main lower-mast

Bluenose replicas) and St. Mary's Bay Industries of Nova Scotia.

By March 13, the deadline for receipt of tenders, five had been received. Included among them was a bid from a yard which had not been approached by the Company. One of the shipbuilders asked to tender had found himself unable to do so and had suggested to Alan Hinks of J. Hinks & Son of Appledore that his firm might be suitable. Hinks had written to the London Office and had been given permission to submit an estimate. Ironically, the Hinks tender of £57,475 was the lowest, and on May 16, 1967, a contract to build the *Nonsuch* was signed between the two companies.

Appledore was an unexpected bonus. This tiny community on the River Torridge in North Devon, just a few miles downstream from Bideford, had a proud connection with the sea that began in 1625, forty-five years before the Company received its founding charter. A milestone in its seafaring history was the development of a thriving timber trade with Canada after 1815, in conjunction with nearby Bideford. Appledore was one of the last British towns to own and operate commercial sailing ships.

While it was considerably junior to the town, J. Hinks & Son had no upstart association with the sea. The firm was established in

19

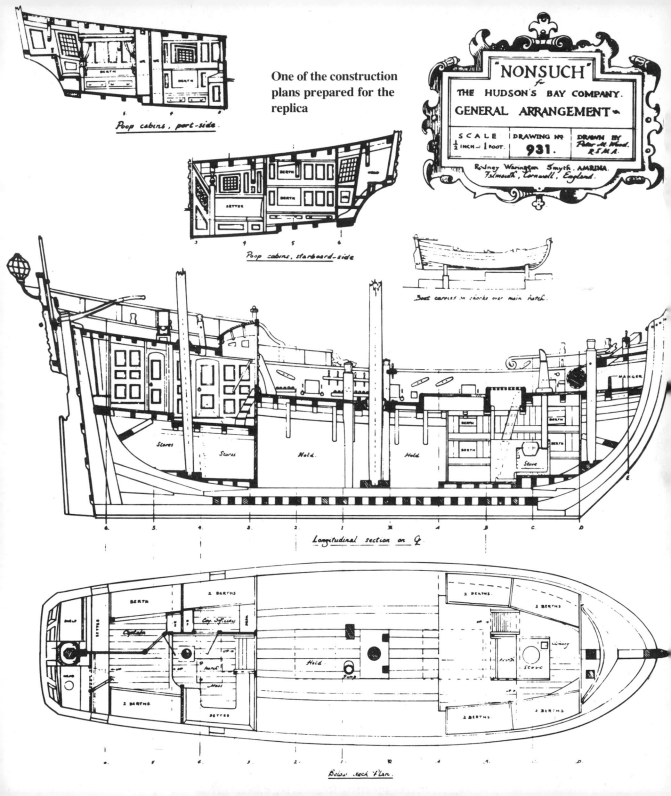

One of the construction plans prepared for the replica

Poop cabins, port-side.

Poop cabins, starboard-side.

"NONSUCH"
for
THE HUDSON'S BAY COMPANY.
GENERAL ARRANGEMENT.

SCALE	DRAWING Nº	DRAWN BY
½ INCH = 1 FOOT.	931.	Peter M. Wood. R.S.M.A.

Rodney Warington Smyth, AMRINA.
Falmouth, Cornwall, England.

Boat carried on chocks over main hatch.

Stores   Stores   Hold.   Hold.   Stove

Longitudinal section on ₵

Below deck Plan.

1844, and in 1851 Henry Hinks was awarded a second prize for the best lifeboat model in the Great Exhibition in London, the contemporary equivalent of a World's Fair. Alan Hinks, a soft-spoken, slight man, was the fourth generation of a family of shipbuilders and an expert at his work. The yard specialized in building strong, conventional vessels, mainly fishing boats and sea-going pleasure craft. Alan Hinks had never attempted a replica, but the ship could not have been in better hands. The painstaking attention to the quality of the work that went into the *Nonsuch* was an important factor in winning Hinks a subsequent contract to reproduce Sir Francis Drake's *Golden Hinde* for American interests.

More than two months passed after the construction contract was signed before the replica was publicly announced, a delay caused by Winnipeg's futile attempt to replace the Manitoba Government's verbal commitment to provide a home for the *Nonsuch* with an official agreement. With words still the Company's only guarantee, the project was announced in Winnipeg and in London on July 20, 1967.

The announcement created considerable publicity and was a help to Alan Hinks, who because of the secrecy of the scheme had been thwarted in his efforts to procure some of the materials he required. Now he could move more freely. His search for a prime specimen of pine for the ship's 45-foot main lowermast ended at Longleat, the Wiltshire estate of the Marquess of Bath. Nearby

The *Nonsuch* replica under construction, with framing complete

Bideford was the source for much of the timber used in the replica: it had nearly formed part of a replica of Captain James Cook's *Endeavour,* the ship in which he discovered Australia, but lack of capital had ended the project, and the seasoned timber was secured by Hinks for the *Nonsuch.*

The ship's cornerstone, the keel, was of English narrow-leaf elm, like the one fitted to the original. When it was laid in October, construction was formally underway, supervised by Mr. Warington Smyth. The project attracted much attention; the shipyard became a community focal point and a tourist attraction. The visitors book was filled with hundreds of signatures not only of British people but of Europeans and Canadians as well.

The specifications for the *Nonsuch* that were given to the builder filled thirty-five pages, constituting a thorough document that read like a set of commandments. They demanded spirit and discipline from all who participated in the project, for the objective was to build a ship that was as nearly as possible a replica of the original ketch *Nonsuch.* Construction was to follow the "maximum possible authenticity," to avoid anachronisms, and "to appreciate fully that the vessel is intended to be a museum piece."

Authenticity required, to some degree, the use of seventeenth-

An apprentice uses a trunnel mute to make the oak pegs (trunnels, or treenails) that will secure the ship's planking to her frame. After the shipwright drives a trunnel through a plank, its inner end is wedged and then sawn flush. The outer end is caulked.

century tools – hand tools such as the adze, the broad axe, the trunnel mute (a kind of round spokeshave specially made from a pattern supplied by the Maritime Museum), and the pane maul (a spoked hammer used to drive trunnels). In the same authentic vein it was necessary to caulk the hull seams with oakum, a practice almost obsolete.

The ship's sails were manufactured by the Lucas Sail Loft of Portsmouth. With the exception of the use of flat seams (a nine-teenth-century innovation) instead of round seams, Lucas displayed accurate, period craftsmanship. Brass eyelets, machine stitching and wire were outlawed; modern fabrics or synthetic fibre were forbidden. The sails were hand-sewn from the best quality Navy flax canvas woven in Scotland, which ranged from fifteen ounces for the jib to twenty-four ounces for the main sail. The mainsail and the staysail were each given a "bonnet," a detachable piece of canvas that could be added to the base of these sails. The sail area, including bonnets, covered 1,957 square feet. (In January 1970 this was increased to 2,147 square feet by the addition of a square spritsail, typical of the period, which the Captain felt would "give some purpose to the rather heavy and bare bowsprit . . . ")

Carvings were characteristic of seventeenth-century ships, and

Photo on the left shows the flax canvas sails being made; centre: Jack Whitehead carves a mermaid under the starboard cathead; far right shows the ship's ornate stern and the windows of the aft cabin.

Jack Whitehead, a carver on the Isle of Wight, and Norman Gaches, his assistant, were assigned the task of adorning the *Nonsuch*. The specifications devoted more than a page to a list of varied subjects to be reproduced singly, in pairs, or in greater quantity. They called for such embellishments as "5 carved gunport wreaths per side," "lion masks on catheads," and "1 life-size crouching dog per side" (later christened Wellington and Boot by the crew). They included details for fruit, flowers, foliage, a magnificently decorated stern and a number of female nudes – apparently to reflect the sailor's belief that an unclothed woman could calm a storm.

Even below deck authenticity prevailed. Conditions on board the original ketch were primitive by today's standards, but not unusual by those of the seventeenth century. Sailors were provided with tiny bunks crowded against the ship's side. Since there were often more sailors than berths, either the men would share, rotating the bunks between watches, or the excess would sleep on deck. The captain and guests did not fare much better; even they had little more than hutches for accommodations. To add to the discomfort, there was no heat, no toilets and only candles or oil lamps for light. Food was prepared in a simple galley and water was strictly rationed. The only compensation for this rigorous life appeared to be

the daily alcohol issue. As late as the 1790's every seaman in the Royal Navy was issued eight pints of beer daily (the normal drink because of the difficulty of preserving water) and a large quantity of spirits.

The Company did not duplicate this uninviting picture entirely. The alcohol ration remained history. The number of paid crew never exceeded the accommodations, and volunteers or guests would have a choice of a hammock, the bench in the captain's cabin, or the decks. An electrical system, a toilet and a serviceable galley were to be installed. Nevertheless, the crew quarters remained as cramped and uncomfortable as they had been centuries before. The bunks resembled coffins – low, narrow, claustrophobic boxes favouring short men. There was no heat except from the galley stove. Fresh air entered through the hatch above the galley table or through the one above the ladder to the forecastle, or fo'c'sle. In rough, wet weather when these were battened down, there was no ventilation at all. On cold days the crew lived in damp discomfort; during the heat of summer, they sweltered. The fo'c'sle had a multiple role: it was where the crew ate and relaxed, and where the majority slept. The crew cohabited with their personal effects, ship's gear, a galley table, two benches, provisions, the galley stove and sink – all shoved into the forward part of the ship, which roughly measured 12 feet by 16 feet. They were virtually room-mates of Winnipeg's victory, the auxiliary engine, which was slightly aft of midships.

By comparison the aft cabin, the captain's quarters, offered spacious comfort. With its pine panelling, brass lanterns, red brocade curtains, multi-paned windows and scarlet H B C 'Point' blankets on the bunks, it had a warmth the fo'c'sle lacked. Euphemistically called the Great Cabin, it was the ship's showpiece, but in fact it was no more than a small room. It seemed larger than it was, simply because it served only a few people.

As the launching date approached, excitement mounted in the yard and enveloped all of Appledore. Finishing touches were put to the ship. Coats of paint and varnish were applied. She was given a white bottom and black wales, and from the gunport mouldings to the top of the rail she was painted a medium blue, to match exactly the colour specified by the experts after examining numerous old prints and paintings. Inside the bulwarks she was painted red; below deck the wood remained natural. Ballast was added. She was fitted with flags and her cannons were primed. Four days before the launching Lord Amory described the preparations as "tremendous," and said that the festivities would be on a par with those for the launching of the Cunard Liner Q.E. II, "with the sole difference that the Queen will not (as far as we know) be present." Invitations had been dispatched and remarks prepared for the Governor. His aunt, Mrs. L. Heathcoat Amory, who had always had a keen interest in her nephew's career and activities, had agreed to christen the ship.

The flurry of activity ended at last when launching day arrived. The people surged forward to see, Mrs. Amory wished Godspeed, champagne drenched the bow and the *Nonsuch* was coaxed into the water. There may have been some who wondered about her future and how she would meet the challenges of the New World; certainly the ship herself seemed to express reluctance to leave the security of the shipyard and face the unknown adventures ahead.

26

"The appointment of a captain is one of the most important operating decisions we will make. Presumably his qualifications will include expert technical sailing skill, ability to command, an attractive personality for press and television coverage and perhaps even some writing ability." Mr. A.R. Huband, secretary to the Canadian Committee in Winnipeg, recognized that a man with such extraordinary qualifications was probably as uncommon as the ship he would command, and he urged an immediate start on recruitment in March 1968. But in the choice of a captain, Winnipeg's ambition to have the *Nonsuch* sail to Canada posed certain problems: Would a British skipper transfer the ship to a Canadian when the ship reached Canada? Could a Canadian be appointed second-in-command? Or perhaps there could be a dramatic handing-over in mid-Atlantic!

And while it would be an advantage to have a commander who could write, it was not, perhaps, a talent that should be over-emphasized: "It would be all very fine," wrote Mr. Murray, "to have a stirring account written of the passage, but I would rather have the ship get safely across under a skipper with a salty, unprintable vocabulary and have the story subsequently ghost-written, than have the ship come to grief in mid-Atlantic with a final distress message sent out in Shakespearean English."

The Company had an idea of what they wanted the *Nonsuch* captain to be, but they lacked the technical knowledge to make the choice themselves. The responsibility of choosing a captain therefore was transferred to the Advisory Committee, a body created by Lord Amory to judge the ship's seaworthiness. The Committee, with Lord Amory as chairman, consisted of three sailing experts: Commander Erroll Bruce, R.N. (Retired), Commander F. Ralph H. Swann, O.B.E., R.N.V.R. (Retired), and Commander Alan J. Villiers, D.S.C., a man of international reputation as a fine author, naval historian and master of the *Mayflower* replica which had crossed the Atlantic to the United States in 1957. The Committee interviewed six men for the master's berth in July, and on July 23, Mr. Adrian Small was appointed Acting Master/Superintendent of the vessel.

In the United Kingdom

The name and person of Adrian Small meant nothing to the Company in Winnipeg. London supplied no photographs and initially sent only minimal information about the man. Although even to prairie people his credentials were obviously those of an experienced seaman, Winnipeg gleaned a less favourable impression from a comment from London that Adrian Small was a humourless fellow who "may hang most of the crew from the yardarm under some Elizabethan authority!" In spite of the intended humour of the remark, the effect was to reduce Captain Small's appeal. Winnipeg wondered if London had made an appropriate choice. From the slim information provided, the man emerged as a dull, colourless chap, a gruff individual with sailing experience his only recommendation. A pleasant surprise awaited Winnipeg.

Adrian Small had heard of a replica being built in the Hinks yard, but on one of his visits to see the project he was told that she was to be manned by Canadians, so he abandoned any thought of serving on her crew. Nevertheless, he continued to follow the construction of the *Nonsuch* closely and found she grew more and more beautiful as the hull rose in the stocks and the carvings came to life.

When the Company advertised the position of master of the *Nonsuch* in several major U.K. dailies, some of Small's friends sent him the ad, suggesting he apply. He took their advice, and since candidates were obliged to come to London for an interview, he bought a new suit. On his way to the Company's London Office, Small was unnerved by a chance meeting with another candidate for the master's berth, a man who Small was convinced would get the job because of his excellent credentials; nevertheless, he went through with the interview. He was ushered into a room and seated at one end of a long table, facing the Governor's Advisory Committee who were off in the distance at the other end. After what seemed an interminable period of silence, he was questioned about his career. To his increasing dismay, one member of the committee made copious notes of each answer.

Despite the presence of his long-time friend Alan Villiers, Small

In the ship's Great Cabin, Captain Adrian Small makes an entry in the Log.

found it a daunting interview. But it turned out to be worth the ordeal, for shortly after leaving the building he happened to meet one of the committee members, who told him he had the job, and his career with the *Nonsuch* began.

Captain Small's qualifications exceeded those penned by Mr. Huband and the man bore no resemblance to London's description. He was thirty-nine years old, a resident of Brixham, married and the father of three. With his full red beard and dressed in period costume, he personified modern man's conception of a seventeenth-century sea captain. While to some people he might have looked somewhat forbidding, he proved to be an engaging gentleman who won countless friends for the Company, the ship and himself. His letters and reports were written in an entertaining, expressive style, and although he disliked public speaking, his remarks were appropriate, enjoyable and often hilarious. His talent as a marine artist (an unexpected extra) was evident in the illustrations he had done for books and magazines published in Britain and Canada.

Although he had an unyielding dedication to detail and duty which sometimes exhausted or irritated his associates or crew, he was rarely too busy to receive unexpected visitors in his cabin. He was known to be late for social functions in port because he always made time for the public, to sign autographs, pose for pictures or make a special fuss over someone on board.

Much of Adrian Small's life had been devoted to the sea, studying maritime history and sailing period ships. He began his career at seventeen as an apprentice aboard the Finnish four-masted marque *Passat* during her voyage around the world from 1946 to 1948 which included an eastward rounding of Cape Horn. After a short hitch in the British Merchant Marine, Small spent several years employed by the film industry, sailing the ships featured in "Billy Budd," "Damn the Defiant" and "Hawaii," among other productions. He had been introduced to this rather glamourous vocation by Captain Villiers in 1954 when the two of them were aboard the *Pequod,* the ship used in the Hollywood version of "Moby Dick," and he had served with Villiers again in 1957 as his second mate on the *Mayflower* replica. When he joined the *Nonsuch* he was recognized as one of the most experienced square-rig sailors in the world.

Captain Small's immediate chore was to select the first crew. He wanted experienced seamen, a qualified engineer, a good cook, and a skilled shipwright or two. He was instructed not to appoint anyone without the Company's approval, but this restriction he largely ignored, and Company executives met some of the crew for the first time at the launching. Small chose men whom he knew personally or by reputation; each was chosen because he was qualified to fill a specific slot. He began to assemble his crew in September.

Mark Myers, a Californian who became the ship's boatswain, was the first to join. He was an experienced square-rig seaman and a talented marine artist as well. He was followed in a few weeks by Clive Gurrin, another qualified seaman, and Alfred Weatherill, Small's neighbour in Brixham and a shareholder in the Hudson's

Bay Company. Mr. Weatherill had no sailing experience, but Small needed a cook, someone in this capacity whom the crew would respect. Engineer David Ayles and Mate Nigel Glassborrow commenced duties on October 23. The following week Robert Cann, one of Hinks' carpenters and an early applicant to join the ship, signed on.

The last member of the original crew was Robert Pearce, a lanky youth of eighteen from Bideford. Pearce had been an apprentice shipwright with Hinks when the firm commenced work on the *Nonsuch,* and he assumed responsibility for manufacturing many of the trunnels used in the replica. He was so fascinated with the vessel that he asked to join her crew, and he remained with the ship, virtually without leave, until her sailing days were through. His first berth on the *Nonsuch* was that of assistant carpenter. To differentiate him from two other Roberts employed by Hinks, his co-workers had nicknamed him "Jam,"a contraction of the English slang expression "jammy" referring to someone with a soft job. On the *Nonsuch* this nickname evolved into "Jan." (North Americans inevitably asked, "After the opera singer?")

The Hinks yard lacked a suitable deep-water berth for the completion of the *Nonsuch's* rig, so while the crew was being mustered she went to Lemay's Yard on the Torridge to be fitted out. The bowsprit was stepped mechanically. The mainmast and mizzen followed, hoisted high and then lowered through the deck openings awaiting them. Then the riggers went into action, swarming aloft to set up the standing rigging. Shrouds and stays appeared, pulling the spars into position, securing them firmly. The heavy canvas sails were bent on, or fastened to their yards. The lofty rig transformed the naked oak hull into a picturesque ketch.

Below deck, an army of shipwrights, fitters and electricians were working, installing the controversial engine designed to keep the ketch on schedule and enable her to manoeuvre in port. As more of the twentieth century was added, the *Nonsuch* became a hybrid, not entirely authentic, but with the modern age kept to a respectable

Lowering the main-mast and maintop into place

and essential minimum. The toilet, water tanks, galley and electrical system were installed. To comply with British Board of Trade requirements she was equipped with contemporary safety equipment, rafts, rings, life-jackets, flares, fire extinguishers and a fog horn. Several tests were taken by the designer and the Board of Trade to gauge the ship's stability. The results were poor. In an attempt to reduce the problem a 12-ton lead keel was added, a slow and difficult procedure undertaken in early October. By the end of the month the lengthy task of fitting out was finished. The Board of Trade inspected the vessel for seaworthiness on November 4 and granted her clearance to sail.

The *Nonsuch* left Appledore on Saturday, November 9, on her maiden voyage, bound for her sea trials at Falmouth. It was the season when westerly gales prevailed. Her course lay along the treacherous Cornish coast, which between Appledore and Falmouth offered no place for a ship to take refuge.

Captain Small had taken every precaution to secure the ship against bad weather, and the vulnerable stern windows were covered with heavy boards to prevent a raging sea from breaking in and flooding the ship. Without knowing how the vessel would handle at sea, the crew left Appledore on the *Nonsuch,* hoping for fine weather.

By dawn the next day, she had successfully rounded dreaded Land's End when her luck changed, and the *Nonsuch* had her first taste of an Atlantic gale. The unclad ladies on the stern of the ship appeared to have no effect, and she began pitching severely; her propeller, offset on the port side, bobbed out of the water occasionally. Seasickness was rife. Lifelines were rigged along the main deck. Because of the offset propeller there was some difficulty steering, and two men were at the helm. When it became necessary to keep the rudder hard over, the entire strength of the watch on deck was needed.

By eight-thirty that morning the *Nonsuch* was 7½ miles off the Lizard, the southernmost point of Great Britain. The rugged coast, pierced with caves and fringed with bold, isolated rocks, was a

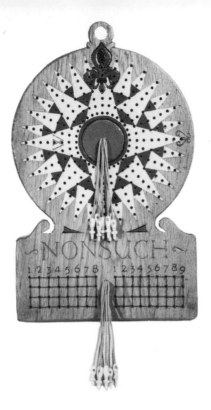

The traverse board

A traverse board was a navigational instrument used from the mid-sixteenth century to the early nineteenth century to record the courses steered by a ship and often the speed of the vessel as well.

Dual purpose traverse boards, such as the one on the *Nonsuch* replica, were divided into two sections. On the instrument designed by Captain Small, the circular upper portion, used to record the ship's course, was decorated by a compass rose with holes arranged in a series of eight concentric circles. The distance between each circle was equal to one half hour; eight half–hour circles, therefore, com-

notorious ships graveyard, and it was evident that the strength of the ketch's engine was insufficient to keep her from being forced dangerously close to the shore. Fortunately, her predicament was spotted and the lifeboat *Lizard Cadgwith* appeared and offered a line. Captain Small accepted, hoping that the extra power would reduce the strain of steering and help keep the ship off the rocks. The *Nonsuch* proceeded under tow around the Lizard.

The lifeboat, in spite of the skill and courage of its men, was not up to the task. In the turbulent sea it was impossible to keep the towline taut. The *Nonsuch* heaved in one direction, the lifeboat in another – the line went limp. Suddenly, the *Nonsuch* plunged ahead, fouling her propeller in the towline and slicing it in two. The lifeboat's crew tried to send aboard another line, but it too was lost. As a last resort the coxswain of the lifeboat used its anchor wire and chain to secure the *Nonsuch* – success! But with the *Nonsuch* prised the traditional four-hour sea watch.

Eight pegs were suspended on cords from the centre of the compass rose. Beginning at the centre ring of holes, a peg would be inserted in the hole corresponding to the compass point being steered by the ship. At the end of each half hour, a peg would be inserted until all eight were employed. The result was a record of the course followed during the four-hour period.

The rectangular lower section of the board was used to record the ship's speed, and it featured four vertical rows of holes separated by eight pegs on individual cords. The left-hand rows, numbered from one to eight, represented distance in fathoms, a fathom being one eighth of a knot. The right-hand rows, numbered from one to nine on the *Nonsuch* board, indicated knots. Every hour a logline would be unreeled from the ship's stern to determine her speed through the water. The number of knots and fathoms indicated were recorded by inserting pegs in the appropriate holes.

At the end of the four-hour watch the pegs were removed, the information on the board might be entered in the log and the same procedure would be repeated for the next four hours. A ship would usually carry a half-hour sand glass to mark the passage of time and a two- or four-hour watch glass.

---

engine out of commission she was a dead weight, and progress toward port was negligible. The two ships pitched in the sea with the lifeboat barely holding its own.

At this point, a third ship arrived on the scene. The Company had been informed of the difficulty and sent a chartered tug, the *Warrior* out of Falmouth, to the rescue.

Small accepted its line and the tug headed toward Falmouth. But the lifeboat's anchor line had jammed on the ketch and its crew were reluctant to cast it off, having lost so many lines already. The three vessels rode the heavy seas linked like sausages. The *Lizard Cadgwith* found itself in the humiliating position of being towed stern first by the very vessel it had attempted to aid, until at last the line was parted by a *Nonsuch* crewman wielding a hacksaw. The lifeboat returned to its base, its lines lost, anchor chain broken and pride wounded. The cost of the damaged or lost gear was assumed by the

Company, and the members of the lifeboat's crew were given a gratuity in appreciation for their service.

The *Warrior* brought the *Nonsuch* safely into Falmouth, where the following weekend the Advisory Committee held a post-mortem on the inaugural run. The Captain and crew were commended for their actions. The passage had revealed minor defects in the period windlass, the pump, the companionways and the steering, and the Committee recommended improvements. But they also recommended that the Company accept the ship; in their opinion she was well built, and the minor weaknesses which had been detected were not the fault of the builder. When the meeting adjourned, the *Nonsuch* commenced twelve days of sea trials that were really redundant after the challenges of her maiden voyage.

The ship's base for the trials was a buoy in Falmouth Harbour and the principal test area was the Carrick Roads, an elongated stretch of deep water with Falmouth on the west and St. Mawes on the east. Above these two ports were several creeks; Mylor, the first one on the west side, provided the small harbour where the *Nonsuch* spent her first winter, watched by a skeleton crew. She was in the vicinity of several associates: Mr. Warington Smyth, whose charming old house stood nearby; Mr. Wilfred Grossmith, who made a traverse board (designed by Captain Small) and a common log and presented them to the ship; and Mr. R.E. Hardy, who fashioned a cross-staff to add to the vessel's collection of period navigational instruments.

During that short cold winter the aft section of the ship below deck was redesigned to reduce the congestion. The aft quarters had originally been divided by a bulkhead, with the port side occupied by the captain's quarters and the starboard side by the ship's toilet. The bulkhead was removed and the toilet relocated across from the engine approximately amidships. The stern bench was extended to the full width of the aft cabin and the captain's bunk was duplicated on the starboard side for use by the mate. Further forward in the cabin a small chart-table was built, with lockers beneath.

Stern and port side
view of the *Nonsuch*
under sail shortly after
being fitted out

That same winter the Company took possession of the shallop, built by the Hinks yard at a cost of £2,460. It was fashioned after a small type of boat often used by early explorers to survey uncharted coastlines, harbours or rivers where it was unwise to take the mother ship, but it had been modernized by the installation of an auxiliary engine. Although Winnipeg had seen no justification for a shallop, it had not rejected the idea flatly when Mr. Warington Smyth proposed it, but asked to reserve judgment until the captain of the *Nonsuch* had been appointed and his thoughts on this matter were known. Captain Small, however, had not been consulted, and the subject had not been raised with Winnipeg again. London had placed the order in September 1968.

It was the Company's original intention to operate the *Nonsuch* in Canada during 1969 and 1970, and at the end of this period to bring her to Winnipeg. That plan changed in April 1968. During the construction stage, the London office discovered that the *Nonsuch* was attracting considerable attention and believed there would be acute disappointment unless she was exhibited in the U.K. prior to her departure for Canada; Winnipeg supported the change of plan.

Throughout the summer of 1969, the *Nonsuch* was displayed in several places along the south coast, and just before the end of the season she crossed the English Channel to Cherbourg, France. Arrangements for the tour were the responsibility of Commander Peter Winter, R.N., hired by the Company as the ship's public relations officer. His methods gave the Company in Winnipeg the foundation upon which to build summer tours for the ship in Canada. He made all the dock and shore arrangements for the ship and crew, alerted the press and co-ordinated the ship's in-port activities. He often found himself rendering services beyond the call of duty, in such diverse occupations as ship's night-watch man, the Captain's private secretary, and mailman to the crew.

Commander Winter's approach was to have the *Nonsuch* moored alongside a quay or some other place where people could pass close to her, so that the ship's low free-board would afford the public a view of her intriguing deck. Occasionally the Company held

Passing under Tower Bridge, London, April 1969

small receptions on the ship, or arrangements were made for groups to come on board for a talk by the Captain. It was the general practice, however, not to admit the public, because of the ship's small size and unavoidably cluttered deck.

As a rule, the ship's official visits lasted about a week to ten days in each port, but the *Nonsuch* was in London from April 21 to May 28, the longest stop of the summer. Nine days at Greenwich followed. In more than a month the ship moved only twice. Nevertheless the crew – particularly Small who was confirmed the vessel's captain during the London stop – were not idle, for they spent marathon days entertaining people on board for the Company. The ship's log shows that an estimated 17,467 visitors saw the *Nonsuch* in these two ports.

It was the opinion of the Company's London Office that public interest in the *Nonsuch* "never flagged" during her stays in London and Greenwich, but it is doubtful that the same could be said for the crew. They rarely enjoyed prolonged, immobile visits that offered

little diversion from playing host to countless visitors and selling booklets about the ship. It was a tedious routine, and the men grew restless for a change of pace, anxious for a day under sail. Their impatience was not mollified by the period costumes they were required to wear when guests were on board or when the ship was on public view. Official dress consisted of six basic parts: black buckled shoes, woollen knee-socks, baggy woollen breeches, loose-fitting shirts with billowing sleeves and various styles of jerkins and hats.

Captain Small questioned the authenticity of these garments. He considered the crew of the replica infinitely better outfitted than their seventeenth-century counterparts, who would have had little more than filthy rags to wear. The costumes were heavy, and although they offered perfect protection against sub-zero weather, this thermal quality was grossly out of season in summer. But the chief complaint about the costumes was that they were a safety hazard. There was always the chance that those itchy, baggy, floppy garments would catch on something, possibly with unfortunate results.

The costumes, however, were not the cause of what was the only major crew mishap suffered on the *Nonsuch*. Strangely enough, it happened at a time when the crew were in high spirits for they were leaving the suffocating stops on the Thames. The ship was operating with a reduced crew; men had been paid off at their own request or because they were not needed in London. One of these vacancies was filled by P.W. Coke, an older man who had been with the ship at Mylor and rejoined her the morning she left for Greenwich. Nine days later, shortly after the *Nonsuch* departed from Greenwich, Bill Coke was dragged the length of the poop, his foot caught in a loop in the shallop towline which was being let out; it jammed hard against the fairlead at the stern of the ship. His foot could not be saved; eventually it had to be amputated above the ankle.

The ship's final major passage in the U.K. rivalled the adventure of her maiden voyage. Again, she had to make a winter passage around the Lizard and along the Cornish coast, but this time it was from Exeter to the Charles Hill & Son Shipyard at Bristol, where she would be prepared for her crossing to Canada. She left her snug winter berth at the Exeter Maritime Museum on January 22, 1970, and almost immediately struck bad weather. A gale delayed the ship for two days at the Exmouth end of the Exeter Canal. She made her way to Falmouth, via Brixham, where she arrived just ahead of another gale which stormed the port on January 30. She remained weather bound in Falmouth until February 10, when, on a good forecast, she set sail for Bristol.

She was rigged for a winter passage: her topsails and topmasts had been struck and her sail plan reduced to the mainsail, lateen, main staysail, jib and spritsail; a bonnet was on the staysail only. She made good progress on February 11. At one point she travelled eighteen miles in two hours, causing her jubilant crew to congratulate themselves on what promised to be a fast passage to Bristol. Although several miles remained, the *Nonsuch* was now well into the Bristol Channel.

Shortly after midnight Captain Small learned that Avonmouth and Bristol were closed by a dock strike. ''The wind was piping up from the east,'' noted the Captain, and gales were forecast. He requested a berth at Barry on the south coast of Wales, and asked for a pilot. About an hour later the *Nonsuch* was 3½ miles southwest of Barry but was making no headway against the wind. The Barry pilot arrived and was told *Nonsuch* was turning to the west as the ship could not make Barry on the present tide. The pilot returned to Barry and the *Nonsuch* headed toward the wider reaches of the Channel, for as long as she stayed clear of land there was no danger.

Conditions worsened. The wind rose to gale force and at one point reached an estimated Force 9 (47-54 m.p.h. in statute miles). For eleven hours the storm unleashed its worst. The ship rode well, plunging and rolling considerably, but shipping little sea on deck. A freezing spray, however, drove relentlessly across the ship. Visibility was poor; it was impossible to look to windward or to keep dry

Battling the Bristol Channel storm in March 1970

despite, wrote Captain Small, "old tricks like 'soul & body' lashings, towels round the necks & waist, socks as gloves . . . ." Few bunks remained dry; the wettest part of the ship was the chart-table which was adjacent to a small starboard window with a poorly-fitting plug. Although the window was caulked with rags, "seawater was squirting in like a hose & soaking the chart." Throughout it all, normal watches were maintained; at each change of watch "all hands were mustered & accounted for." It was impossible to cook meals but somehow Alfred Weatherill made hot soup and sandwiches to keep the crew in good spirits.

On land there was acute concern that the *Nonsuch* was missing, and national broadcasts in Canada alarmed the Company in Winnipeg with the news. There had been no radio contact with the ship since the storm began. During the morning of February 12 the crew began to hear messages on the ship's radio indicating that an alert or search was underway for the *Nonsuch* and another vessel. The ship's reports had gone unheard; for with the main topmast taken down for the passage, the radio aerial was lower and the broadcast range had been reduced.

The *Nonsuch* was quite safe. That afternoon Captain Small declined offers of assistance, and did so with particular emphasis when two vessels appeared, "one a pilot vessel with press and T.V. on board, the other the Minehead Lifeboat." He was suspicious of the way the press manoeuvered the lifeboat into position to afford dramatic pictures of what would look like a rescue scene. The *Nonsuch* reached Barry at midnight, unescorted and unassisted. The rest of the passage was completed without incident, and by the afternoon of St. Valentine's Day, she was moored at the Charles Hill & Son jetty. She had covered a distance of 273 miles (of which 62 miles were due to the gale), and held her own against the elements like a true descendant of those spirited square-riggers of the past. Her association with the U.K. was now virtually over. In a matter of days she would embark for Canada.

While the *Nonsuch* was getting a taste of salt water in England, Company executives on both sides of the Atlantic were discussing her next move.

Winnipeg had always wanted her to sail to Canada. The organizers of the Canadian tour were not blind to the possible dangers, but they preferred to dream of the tremendous publicity advantages. Such a crossing would be a public relations coup, something like the first moon landing; its potential positively dazzled a promoter's mind. The anaemic alternative was to transport the ship to Canada and run the risk of ridicule – Winnipeg suspected that the press might have great fun pointing to the Company with headlines that asked, "Where are Today's Adventurers?"

The entire Company shared Winnipeg's enthusiasm for a crossing by sail, but everyone recognized that such a weighty decision could not be made without careful consideration, requiring tests, trials, studies, inspections and observations. Twelve months after the ship was launched all the necessary data had been accumulated, and the final reports of the Advisory Committee, the designer and other well-informed people had been received in London. Their conclusions were incorporated in a recommendation which went before the Company Board urging that the *Nonsuch* be transported to Canada rather than attempt the Atlantic crossing on her own.

From a practical point of view the decision was irrefutable. The *Nonsuch* had originally been conceived as a museum piece, but during the research and design phase she had gradually developed into something more than this, and when she was launched, she was a sailing vessel. Subsequently, repeated efforts were made to make her even more seaworthy. In the U.K. her sailing rig was clearly defined for each type of passage she was likely to make. For inshore waters and harbours she could sail with her full rig (with cannons stowed below), but on coastal passages the rig had to be reduced, and the topmasts came down. To the frustrated Captain this meant that the *Nonsuch* "could not leave harbour with enough sail to sail . . . as the topmasts were to be sent down each time." Despite extra

The 1970 Tour

The St. Lawrence and Lake Ontario

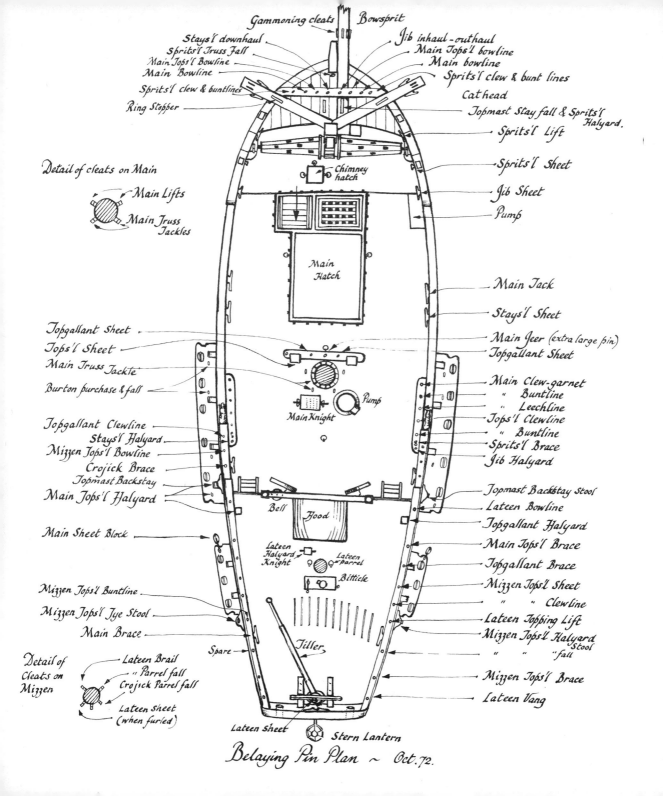

Gammoning cleats   Bowsprit

Stays'l downhaul
Sprits'l Truss Fall
Main Tops'l Bowline
Main Bowline
Sprits'l clew & buntlines
Ring Stopper

Jib inhaul - outhaul
Main Tops'l bowline
Main bowline
Sprits'l clew & bunt lines
Cat head
Topmast Stay fall & Sprits'l Halyard.
Sprits'l Lift
Sprits'l Sheet
Jib Sheet
Pump

Chimney hatch

Detail of cleats on Main
Main Lifts
Main Truss Tackles

Main Hatch

Main Jack
Stays'l Sheet
Main Jeer (extra large pin)
Topgallant Sheet

Topgallant Sheet
Tops'l Sheet
Main Truss Tackle
Burton purchase & fall

Main Knight

Pump

Main Clew-garnet
" Buntline
" Leechline
Tops'l Clewline
" Buntline
Sprits'l Brace
Jib Halyard

Topgallant Clewline
Stays'l Halyard
Mizzen Tops'l Bowline
Crojick Brace
Topmast Backstay
Main Tops'l Halyard

Bell   Hood

Topmast Backstay Stool
Lateen Bowline
Topgallant Halyard
Main Tops'l Brace
Topgallant Brace
Mizzen Tops'l Sheet
" " Clewline
Lateen Topping Lift
Mizzen Tops'l Halyard Stool
" " " fall

Main Sheet Block

Lateen Halyard Knight
Lateen parrel
Bitticle

Mizzen Tops'l Buntline
Mizzen Tops'l Tye Stool
Main Brace

Detail of cleats on Mizzen

Spare   Tiller

Lateen Brail
" Parrel fall
Crojick Parrel fall
Lateen sheet (when furled)

Mizzen Tops'l Brace
Lateen Vang

Lateen Sheet   Stern Lantern

Belaying Pin Plan ~ Oct. 72.

ballast on the keel – twelve tons applied in Appledore and another six in Bristol in order that the ship could sail with her topmasts – the *Nonsuch*'s stability remained questionable. The condition was caused by a lack of beam – Captain Small believed ''3 feet wider would have made all the difference'' – compared to the height and weight of the masts, sails and rigging.

Winnipeg was disappointed with the decision, but did not take issue with it, aware that the two-month voyage would have bitten heavily into the planned summer tour. Still sensitive to the possibility that the press might treat the piggy-back crossing as a joke, a mock symbol of the modern Company's spirit of adventure, Winnipeg chose not to publicize the voyage. Company executives also decided against greeting her arrival in Montreal with even so much as a token fanfare, but for altogether different reasons.

In the fall of 1969 the Company had made the broad decision to exhibit the *Nonsuch* in eastern Canada between Montreal and Toronto, a choice based on commercial and promotional considerations. The region was a new one for the Company's retail opera-

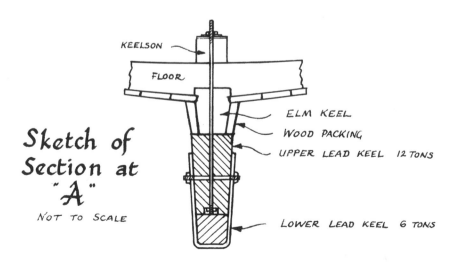

Sketch of Section at "A"

NOT TO SCALE

KEELSON

FLOOR

ELM KEEL

WOOD PACKING

UPPER LEAD KEEL 12 TONS

LOWER LEAD KEEL 6 TONS

A cross-section of the ship's keel, showing the extra lead added to improve her stability

47

tions, and the anticipated public and media response would give the Company a spectacular opportunity to increase awareness of its presence in the heart of Canada's biggest market.

But beginning in 1968, and increasingly throughout 1969, Montreal was the target for demonstrations, bombings and bomb threats, manifestations of the resentment of French-Canadian extremists toward English Canada, particularly the English in Montreal.

The violence subsided significantly in the last few months of the year, but the residual effect remained. It was the opinion of many people that the least provocation might ignite the fire again, and some of them thought the *Nonsuch* might be just such a catalyst. They believed that the ship, with her British trappings and craftsmanship, and the English tradition of her owner, could provoke a negative reaction among some French-Canadians and be damaged, or destroyed. They advised the Company not to bring her to Montreal.

A further problem existed within the Hudson's Bay Company itself. The Company at that time conducted its retail operations in Montreal under the name Morgan's, having purchased the Morgan's retailing chain in 1960. The *Nonsuch* was not considered an asset by the Morgan's management. To be associated with the ship, they felt, could reverse the acceptance that Morgan's, once a solid English carriage trade chain, was beginning to achieve with French-speaking Canadians.

Faced with the double-edged problems posed by Montreal, the Company considered its options: operate the ship exclusively in Ontario; ship her to British Columbia; or deliver the *Nonsuch* to James Bay in response to petitions from residents of Northern Ontario, who leaned heavily on the historical argument that the replica should operate in the territory where the original ship dropped anchor. Each choice had a supporting list of pros and cons, but none offered the Company the value of a *Nonsuch* tour through eastern Canada. To the Company, it dwarfed the risk involved. London was instructed to ship the *Nonsuch* to Montreal.

Onto the deck of the *Bristol City* for the passage to Canada

The *Nonsuch* made her final passage in Britain, a six-mile journey from Bristol to Avonmouth, on March 24. Without her yards, canvas, rigging, and masts, she looked much as she had the day she was launched, except that she was now a motorized hull. The next day she was placed over an iron cradle, custom-made to conform to her hull. Cradle and ship were hoisted out of the water, swung slowly through the air and secured to the deck of the S.S. *Bristol City*. Accompanied by Captain Small, Bos'n Myers, Seamen Jan Pearce and Philip Rose-Taylor (who had joined the ship in January), the *Nonsuch* left for Canada on March 26 – destination Montreal.

Captain Small with Montreal's Mayor Jean Drapeau

The decision to bring the ship to Montreal was only superficially courageous, for it was accompanied by much caution and conservatism. The Company modified its goal for the *Nonsuch* in Quebec to one of limited exposure. It designated Montreal her single official stop in the province, and made the visit conditional upon arranging to exhibit her at Man and His World, formerly Expo 67, the closest thing to neutral ground in troubled Montreal. The Company also decided against refitting the *Nonsuch* in Montreal, and in February, 1970, launched an anxious search for a hideaway harbour or shipyard outside the city. Sorel, forty miles east of Montreal on the south shore of the St. Lawrence, provided the needed sanctuary, and after arriving in Montreal, the *Nonsuch* travelled there under motor power to spend seven pleasant weeks. She was front-page news when she returned to Montreal on June 1 and was welcomed by a touch of pomp and circumstance and Mayor Jean Drapeau. She spent a full month at Man and His World and left unscathed.

But Montreal was not the only question mark facing the Company that summer. The entire tour was a giant guess, planned with crossed fingers and prayers that somehow it would work. Unlike the London office, Winnipeg had no one with Commander Winter's qualifications organizing the tour. Of the people involved with the planning function, only one had even seen the *Nonsuch;* none had any practical knowledge of the ship, the St. Lawrence, Lake Ontario or navigation in general. They had no idea what effect the strong St. Lawrence current would have on the ship's progress upriver, and they could only give approximations in response to the first question asked by members of a clock-watching society "What will be her exact time of arrival?"

Captain Shaw was available occasionally to contribute his nautical experience, and some valued assistance came from the Toronto Brigantine Inc. organization. But even they were stumped by questions like, How much time should be allowed for a seventeenth-century ketch to pass through the locks on the St. Lawrence Seaway? Or, of greater mystery, How would such a little vessel react in these locks? Would the turbulence toss her against the sides like so much driftwood? Would she therefore need a tug, or could she simply be fendered or padded? No one knew the answers, for it had never been done before; even Captain Small could only surmise the outcome as he had no experience in Canadian waters.

By the time the Company and the Captain met to establish a schedule for the tour, the Company had made commitments for the *Nonsuch* at a number of communities along the St. Lawrence and the Canadian shore of Lake Ontario, beginning in Montreal and ending in Toronto. In each community a committee was ready to reserve accommodations for the crew, plan a party, alert the press and help with the numerous details of the ship's visit to their town once the dates were known.

All the ports on the ship's itinerary had been visited by representatives of the Company, who inspected the harbour facilities and verified that the depth of water was sufficient to accommodate the ship. Everything appeared to be in order, until Winnipeg learned that extra lead had been added to the ship's keel in Bristol, increasing her draft and requiring that all the harbour depths be rechecked. While the *Nonsuch* and her crew relaxed at Man and His World, Captain Small visited the ports on the St. Lawrence that lay between Montreal and Kingston. He had no sailing experience on the St. Lawrence, but he had a practised eye and he had read books, consulted knowledgeable people and asked endless questions about what to expect. It was clear to him that the water in many of the harbours was shallow, offering only a fraction more than the depth required by the *Nonsuch,* and he knew that the charted depths were unreliable; but he was persuaded by the Company to agree to visiting these towns against his better judgment. Once the itinerary was settled, he determined to get the ship into every port, although he fully expected to have to drag the ship over the bottom in some of them.

The *Nonsuch* left Cornwall early on the morning of July 4, at the end of a busy three-day stop. She proceeded up the St. Lawrence, and soon she was under full sail, taking advantage of a favourable wind. She looked her magnificent best as she approached Upper Canada Village – all sails set and stiff with wind, her colourful hull gleaming in the afternoon sunshine. Captain Small signalled for cannon salutes to be delivered. Crowds of people hurried to the riverbank, and followed the *Nonsuch* as if she were the Pied Piper as she made her way toward Crysler Park Marina.

Just off the marina entrance, the riverbed and the keel met; the ship struck hard and fast. To the spectators on the shore, the *Nonsuch* was still apparently under sail, and everything seemed normal. But as the ship's position and angle remained constant, they began to realize what had happened.

This adhesive arrival took place in late afternoon, and the day ended with the *Nonsuch* safe, but stranded. By sundown, Captain Small had been joined by Captain John Butt, the senior marine officer for the St. Lawrence Seaway Authority in its Cornwall headquarters. It was July 4, and the American holiday lowered Captain Butt's hopes for help from a Seaway vessel. But luck was not on vacation and by about two o'clock the following morning, the *Nonsuch* was afloat again, as a result of a rise in the water level, increased wind, and the turbulence caused by a passing ship which helped to rock the stranded ketch free. At dawn she was anchored inside the marina.

At eleven o'clock on July 6, the *Nonsuch* weighed anchor inside Crysler Park Marina and departed on schedule for Prescott. She proceeded out of the harbour under engine power at a speed of two knots, with all sails furled. Fifteen minutes later she was aground. Soundings showed a seven-foot depth on the port side, but deeper water to starboard and to the stern of the ship. The bilge was sounded too and revealed that the ship was not taking water. It was a firm grounding in mud and sand.

Captain Butt was recalled. Before returning to the ship, he dispatched a Seaway workboat to the rescue, but while the crew were awaiting its arrival, they attempted to dislodge the *Nonsuch* themselves. First, they lightened her by unloading four tons of ballast and cannons which were taken to shore in the shallop. Then they laid out an auxiliary, or kedge, anchor to windward, and using the windlass as a winch, attempted to pull the ship toward it in order to free the keel. Their efforts were fruitless.

Shortly after four that afternoon, Seaway Workboat No. 115 arrived, followed minutes later by another vessel, the *Island Queen*, whose volunteer services were accepted. Stern lines were taken by both rescue boats, and in less than twenty minutes (with some help from the men on board who, at Captain Small's ringing command, ran from side to side to rock the ship), the *Nonsuch* was at anchor in deep water. Divers reported that her keel was unharmed, but her eight-foot solid oak tiller, was in pieces. As the ship was being towed, the tiller had swung abruptly to starboard and smashed against the railing of the poop. A spare tiller was brought into use and served the ship throughout the rest of her sailing says.

On its own, the day's work provided the men on the *Nonsuch* with an unforgettable experience. Eight days later those memories were given a more frightening cast when the Great Lakes freighter *Eastcliffe Hall* ran aground and sank, just 42 feet from where the *Nonsuch* had grounded. Six men were drowned.

Within a week of the drama at Crysler Park Marina the *Nonsuch* was aground again, this time at the Brockville Yacht Club. The club had·arranged a sail-past for the second evening of her visit, to bring the event to a rousing and historical conclusion, the *Nonsuch* was scheduled to be the last vessel. It seemed an easy assignment. The Company was represented in the official reviewing party which included the mayor of Brockville, the president of the local chamber of commerce and the commodore of the yacht club.

The reviewing party took its place and the sail-past commenced. The commentary over the public address system favoured the *Nonsuch* and was full of laudatory remarks about the ketch, about "the valiant vessel that sailed to Canada three hundred years ago," about the "faithful replica here tonight," about how she had weathered the test of the Bristol Channel storm and how skilful were her crew. While the comments entertained the official party and the people near the reviewing platform, they went largely unheard by the majority of the huge crowd in attendance. Like metal to a magnet, they had been drawn toward the *Nonsuch* and were engrossed by the sight of the "gallant" vessel, stuck in the riverbed at her dock. In a desperate attempt to free her, she had been hitched to a vintage jeep. The four-wheeled museum piece groaned and strained, and finally, tugged the ship loose, amid cheers and applause from the surrounding crowd.

The delay was humiliating but well timed. The *Nonsuch* reached the river just as the last group of boats were setting off to pass in review. She was scheduled to fire a six-gun salute when she was off the reviewing stand. Her cannons impressed everyone. The salvo thundered through town, causing screams of fright, shaking windows, and with each firing, sending the *Nonsuch* pitching back and forth like a deranged rocking horse. The cannons were an effective finale and more than made up for the embarrassment of the grounding. They had been double charged!

Nine times the *Nonsuch* took the ground in 1970. These incidents embarrassed Captain Small, as they would any experienced sea captain, but to a gentleman dedicated to displaying a unique ship to her best advantage these episodes were deeply upsetting. It was some comfort that the ship was not in dangerous or rocky waters where damage might be done. Captain Small's temperament helped too. As the frequency of the groundings increased, he dryly suggested that the Company should not stand in the way of the ship's fondness for land but encourage it, and avoid the possible perils of the St. Lawrence bottom by attaching wheels to the hull and driving her from port to port.

During the career of the *Nonsuch* there was never a lack of applicants to join her crew, but there was a constant shortage of people who knew sailing ships. In 1970 the *Nonsuch* had aboard a disproportionate number of inexperienced men.

Bos'n Mark Myers had left the *Nonsuch* following her month at Man and His World, but the rest of the nucleus crew who accompanied the ship to Canada remained throughout the summer. The services of Captain Small and Messrs. Rose-Taylor and Pearce had been supplemented by five other men. Two came from Winnipeg: Hugh Swan and Samuel Richards were selected from over eighty applications the Company received in the city; both men joined as ordinary seamen. Other members of the 1970 crew included David Epp and Robert Hunter of Toronto, and Paul Cunningham of Fredericton, New Brunswick. The crew was occasionally augmented throughout that and future summers by Sea Cadets chosen from the Corps which often assisted the *Nonsuch* in port.

For the men of the *Nonsuch* life with the ship was a bittersweet mix of luxury and hardship. They had the opportunity, the accidental good fortune in some cases, to sail on a unique ship. In most North American and English ports the ship visited on a scheduled basis, the Company provided the crew with hotel rooms, accommodations as near the ship as possible which ran the gamut of desirability, from Toronto's posh Royal York Hotel to its most sleazy opposite. Those members of the crew who did not qualify for Canadian medical programs had their hospital bills covered by the Company. (It was not an expensive scheme for it incurred only one major bill – a circumcision required by one of the more experienced U.K. members of the crew. He claimed that in his home country the operation would not have cost him a cent; the Company maintained that since the need for the operation did not arise because of his work on the *Nonsuch*, it would only share the cost.) The Captain was provided

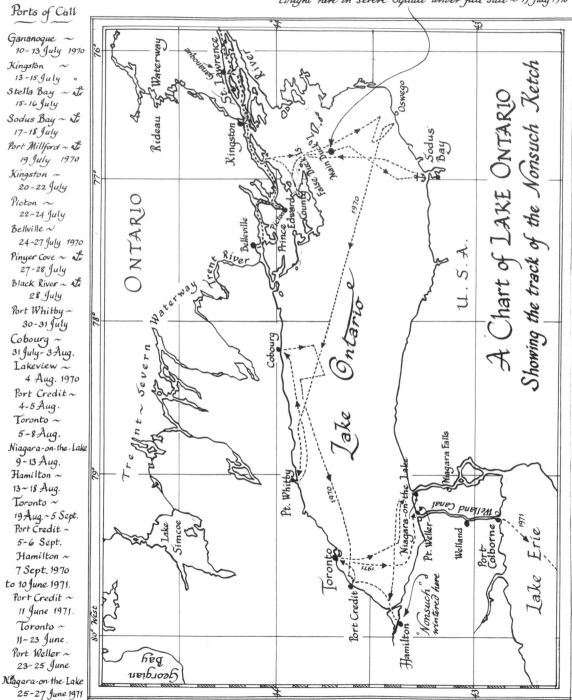

Ports of Call

Gananoque ~
10-13 July 1970

Kingston ~
13-15 July "

Stella Bay ~ ⚓
15-16 July

Sodus Bay ~ ⚓
17-18 July

Port Millford ~ ⚓
19 July 1970

Kingston ~
20-22 July

Picton ~
22-24 July

Bellville ~
24-27 July 1970

Pinyer Cove ~ ⚓
27-28 July

Black River ~ ⚓
28 July

Port Whitby ~
30-31 July

Cobourg ~
31 July-3 Aug.

Lakeview ~
4 Aug. 1970

Port Credit ~
4-5 Aug.

Toronto ~
5-8 Aug.

Niagara-on-the-Lake
9-13 Aug.

Hamilton ~
13-18 Aug.

Toronto ~
19 Aug.-5 Sept.

Port Credit ~
5-6 Sept.

Hamilton ~
7 Sept. 1970
to 10 June 1971.

Port Credit ~
11 June 1971.

Toronto ~
11-23 June.

Port Weller ~
23-25 June

Niagara-on-the-Lake
25-27 June 1971

*"Nonsuch" and the Brigantine "St. Lawrence II"
caught here in severe Squall under full sail ~ 17 July 1970*

A Chart of LAKE ONTARIO
Showing the track of the Nonsuch Ketch

ONTARIO

U.S.A.

Lake Ontario

Lake Erie

Georgian Bay

Lake Simcoe

Rideau Waterway

Trent ~ Severn Waterway

Trent River

St. Lawrence River

Gananoque

Kingston

Belleville

Prince Edward County

False Duck I.s

Main Duck I.

Oswego

Sodus Bay

Cobourg

Pt. Whitby

Toronto

Port Credit

Hamilton

Niagara-on-the-Lake

Niagara Falls

Pt. Weller

Welland

Welland Canal

Port Colborne

"Nonsuch" wintered here

76°

77°

78°

79°

80° West

1970

1971

1961

Notes: The lifts reeve through a block at bowsprit end & back to the forward pinrail.
The braces lead to a block under the main top & down to the main pinrails.
The Truss tackle sets up at the stem on a cleat
The Halyard reeves through a block under the bowsprit end & back to the pinrail.
The Cleat is on the fore side.
The Footropes, Stirrups & Brace Pendants are served.

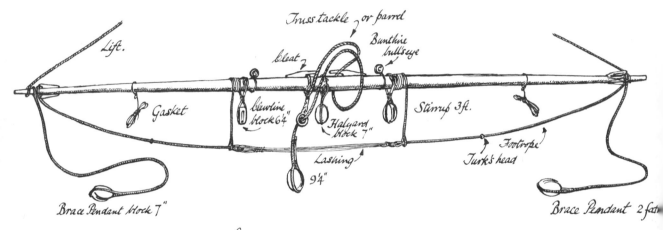

Truss tackle or parrel

Bunthine bullseye

Lift.

Cleat

Gasket

Clewline block 6¼"

Halyard block 7"

Lashing 9¼"

Stirrup 3 ft.

Turk's head

Footrope

Brace Pendant block 7"

Brace Pendant 2 fat

Spritsail Yard

Length o.a.
Max. dia.   6"
Dia. at cleats 2½"

This yard was made at Exeter in January 1970 by the ship's carpenter.

Nonsuch
Seattle, October 1972

56

with a per diem rate per man to feed the crew and any ship's guests; the amount varied according to whether the ship was in port or at sea. Without spending a nickel of the good wages they were paid, the crew could eat quite well on their food allowance, and a few enterprising souls even managed to stretch it to buy themselves some personal effects as well. The crew were virtually wards of the Hudson's Bay Company all the time they were with the ship.

The other side of the picture was less appealing. The *Nonsuch* was not a luxury launch; she was a cramped ketch which offered communal living as her only class of accommodation. None of the *Nonsuch* tours bore any resemblance to a pleasure cruise, for there were always the gruelling pressures of timetables and the dizzy round of publicity engagements. Solitude became a rare treasure. Each summer the crew was sought after for autographs, honoured with dinners, luncheons and receptions, showered with praise. Every season the people came in droves and bombarded the crew with the same questions again and again. The crew of 1970, however, faced additional problems.

The young crew, the Canadians in particular, were rudely awakened to the fact that the tour was not a summer lark, but serious business, and they struggled to cope with its demands. They were frustrated by their responsibilities which gave them little spare time to see the places the ship visited or mingle with people their own age. They looked upon the Captain as a stern father, and referred to him disrespectfully as "the old man." They found him unapproachable, demanding and authoritarian, and often took their questions and complaints to the Company instead.

Captain Small had problems of his own. He was twice the average age of his crew; he knew there was a substantial generation gap on board, but was not confident that he could close it by himself. He sorely missed someone with the qualities of Alfred Weatherill, his invaluable cook and administrative helper, who although even older than Small was respected by the crew yet considered by them to be "one of the boys."

Captain Small was frustrated by the tour pressures, the repeated groundings and his role as a celebrity which he detested. But most of all, he was exasperated by his crew, of whom two-thirds were green and whose appearance he found deplorable. Others felt the same. One visitor to the ship informed the Company that he was confronted by a member of the crew who "but for a pair of short shorts, a belt with a big dagger attached to it at his right hip, a tousled mop of dark hair and considerable beard, was *naked* – not even shoes on his feet!" Their long hair, beards and bare feet were compatible with the baggy period costumes. In their civvies or work clothes, however, the general appearance of the crew was slovenly. The crew had gone to seed. The Captain grappled unsuccessfully with this problem, always afraid that if it was not solved the reputation of the ship and the Company would suffer.

Relief from the daily routine of the tour was planned for Kingston, where the *Nonsuch* would spend a week sailing on Lake Ontario. She would be in the company of the *St. Lawrence II,* a sail training brigantine based in Kingston. For the *Nonsuch* crew, the Lake Ontario cruise would end seventeen consecutive days on tour, during which seven communities had been visited, each with a heavy social agenda. It would also be their first opportunity of the summer to turn off the engine, put aside the whistle-stop schedule and do some real sailing.

On July 15, the *Nonsuch* and the *St. Lawrence II* left Kingston. They anchored overnight in Stella Bay, on the south side of Amherst Island. It was hot and calm and the *Nonsuch* crew tried sleeping on deck, but they were driven below by the mosquitoes. The next morning the ships continued their cruise, using full sail. Suddenly the weather changed. The sky turned grey and threatening and the men could see rain and squalls in the distance. The *St. Lawrence II* was about half a mile astern of the *Nonsuch* when, without warning, a squall hit the brigantine and she heeled right over. In preparation for the coming storm, Captain Small ordered the mate to take in the spritsail. It was furled only moments before the squall reached the *Nonsuch* and took her on the beam. The *Nonsuch* heeled over and began churning up the water on the lee side. Further and further over

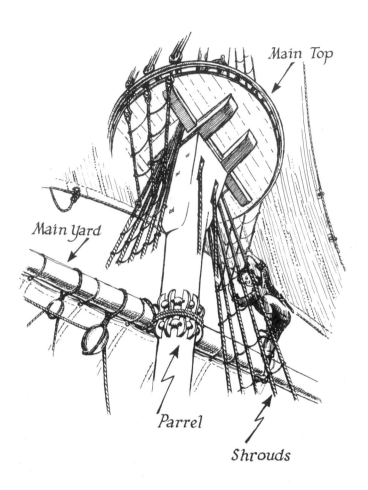

Main Top

Main Yard

Parrel

Shrouds

View of the "Nonsuch" looking aloft at the after side of
the Main mast showing the round Main Top, the
Main yard and the Parrel which holds the yard
to the mast. The seaman climbing aloft holds the
shrouds; his feet are on the "Rattlines." We have replaced
the Parrel with 18th century "Truss tackles." Adrian Small

she went, until the heavy back ends of the cannons tipped up, and Wellington, one of the two carved dogs on the railing, was dipping under the water. The Captain was astounded: it was the biggest roll she had ever done. Captain Small gave orders to take in sail, but the ship was at such an angle that it was all the crew could do to hold on and prevent themselves from sliding down the decks. Inside the ship everything was thrown about. The crew's bedding was soaked by bilge water that came up the ship's sides and into the bunks. The galley crockery suffered sorely.

As quickly as it had come, the squall departed. The two ships sailed on, and next morning anchored in Sodus Bay in Upper New York State. The crew had been up throughout the night sailing the ship, not an undue hardship, but they had been anticipating a hearty breakfast and some sleep upon reaching Sodus Bay. The Captain had opposite ideas. He ordered that all the damp bedding be brought on deck to be aired and dried. When this had been done, he decided it was an excellent opportunity to give the ship a good scrub below. Finally, he announced his intention to sort through each man's clothing and arrange to have the dirty items laundered. The crew grumbled.

Normally even-tempered, Jan Pearce was outraged. He considered the Captain's request a gross invasion of his privacy. He heatedly told the Captain that he did not need assistance in determining which of his clothes needed cleaning; Small replied that if Pearce did not get on with the job he would have to leave the ship when she returned to Kingston. In the end, the Captain inspected only one bag on board. It was one of Pearce's, and the contents were clean. The ship returned to Kingston and the tour resumed.

The growing chasm between the Captain and crew reached its widest point two days later, after the ship's arrival in Picton, when Captain Small refused the crew's request to have guests on board. Pearce, an angry spokesman for about half the crew, informed the Company of their intention to leave the ship in Picton unless something was done to improve the deteriorating state of affairs on board.

The Company was placed in the awkward position of having to mediate a settlement or sacrifice the tour. It would have to become directly involved in the operation of the ship, traditionally a captain's prerogative. It was a delicate situation. Nevertheless, the crew were bluntly told of the captain's problems, of the fears and frustrations he had that summer; and the next morning, the captain was informed of the crew's ultimatum.

He did not take the news placidly. He paced the room furiously, bellowing his rebuttal. *He* was in command of the *Nonsuch*. If the crew did not like the way she was run, if they did not support what he was struggling to accomplish with the ship for the Company, they could either leave or remain on board and suffer the consequences. He seemed dangerously near to becoming the Elizabethan despot London had described, who might hang most of the crew from the yardarm.

Oddly enough, the strained situation at Picton ended undramatically. Like the Lake Ontario squall, it merely died away. No summit meeting was held between Adrian Small and his crew; no mutiny occurred; there was no victory or defeat. "Nothing really changed on board," said Jan Pearce. The problems that existed were not solved that summer, but a subtle change had taken place to reduce the friction between the two parties. The "Sodus Bay Incident" and the confrontation at Picton gave the antagonists a chance to express their grievances, and as a result the air was cleared. This seemed to be all that was necessary. The ship left Picton with a full crew and the tour resumed, with the Captain and crew more of a team because of their deeper understanding of one another.

At Belleville they bid a heartfelt good-bye to the shallop, whose usefulness had reached its peak during the grounding off Crysler Park Marina. During the rest of the tour it had been the ship's albatross, an attractive nuisance that had to be either towed behind the *Nonsuch* or operated by one of the crew because there was no room for it on board. It is unlikely that the original *Nonsuch* carried a shallop on account of her size, and for the purposes of the tour it would have been adequate to hire a tender whenever the need arose.

Period appearance would have been the sole sacrifice. Captain Small left the shallop with RCSCC Quinte, the Sea Cadet Corps in Belleville, for use as a training vessel and the *Nonsuch* sailed away unencumbered.

With the help of her crew, her engine and the elements, the *Nonsuch* had proved a remarkably punctual ship, to the extent that the Company could almost guarantee her arrival time. In 1970 she was only late twice. She arrived in Prescott at the scheduled time, but twenty-four hours late as she had spent the previous day grounded off Crysler Park Marina. Thick haze on the lake reduced visibility and made her fifty minutes late arriving at Niagara-on-the-Lake, but her tardiness did not dampen the enthusiasm that awaited her in port.

This small, rustic community on the Canadian side of the mouth

A typical seventeenth-century shallop

From the maintop,
a view of the
welcoming throng at
Niagara-on-the-Lake

of the Niagara River was the first capital of Upper Canada, and today it enjoys an international reputation for its annual summer festival of the plays of George Bernard Shaw. The town takes justifiable pride in its rich history, and the citizens, many of whose families have lived in the area for generations, work hard to keep the community a charming nineteenth-century period piece, an oasis of the past in this highly developed region of southern Ontario.

The people of Niagara-on-the-Lake grasped the magic of the *Nonsuch* and the potential of the ship's visitation, and enthusiastically exploited it to everyone's advantage. A citizens' committee did considerable promotional work in the community itself, throughout the Niagara Peninsula and across the river in several towns in upper New York State. The *Niagara Advance* kept its readers abreast of the town's plans for the ship, and a few days before her arrival, it published a sixteen-page *Nonsuch* supplement. The town established a special committee which worked for almost five months to develop a full program of historical, religious and social events coincident with the ship's stay.

The *Nonsuch* was escorted into port by a huge welcome flotilla. Dozens of pleasure craft – cruisers, runabouts, tiny dinghies and large sail-boats – were waiting at the mouth of the river when she came into view. The cacophony of boat whistles was punctuated with cannon salutes between the *Nonsuch* and Old Fort Niagara on the American side of the river.

According to the *Niagara Advance,* the crowd that welcomed the *Nonsuch* to Niagara-on-the-Lake was the biggest ever assembled in the town. From the ship it looked as if a sea of humanity covered the Canadian shore. (Captain Small remarked later that it could have been a terrifying sight if all those natives had been unfriendly!) Thousands of Canadians and Americans watched the arrival. The greatest number of people was pressed into the smallest area, the Gillingham Yacht Basin where the official party awaited the ship; the crowd was so dense that it was a struggle to raise an arm or to wave a hand or a flag. There were redcoats and voyageurs from Old Fort Niagara, and costumed members of the Niagara Historical Society. Navy League Wrenettes from Welland and Toronto were present in official dress, and lining the edge of the dock was an honour guard in the crisp white uniforms of the U.S. Naval Reserve Military Training Division at Youngstown, New York.

Long lines of people waited to view the *Nonsuch* each day when she opened to the public, and when she closed, many were turned away. The program of events planned for the crew kept them on a four-day social whirl, attending four dinners, two presentations, a parade and a drumhead service (a religious service held at sundown on the grounds of Fort George). The lord mayor of the town, Fred Goring, visited the ship at least once a day. He purchased one of almost every item for sale in the Nonsuch Shop, a portable – and unprofitable – souvenir shop the Company had developed to accompany the ketch that summer (and which went out of business abruptly in Toronto when a storm blew it into Lake Ontario). Mr. Goring's son took the crew on tours throughout the Niagara Peninsula; a town alderman brought baskets of giant peaches to the ship, freshly picked from his orchard.

The lord mayor and his family and the city fathers were typical of the people of Niagara-on-the-Lake, who were genuinely honoured to have the *Nonsuch* visit their town. They did not use the ship or her crew to selfish ends, as had been the case in some eastern Ontario towns. Here was no grasping harbour-master requesting an

Escorts surround
the *Nonsuch* as
she approaches
Niagara-on-the-Lake,
August 9, 1970

HBC "Point" blanket in return for connecting an extension cord to
operate the ship's lights. In exchange for the visit, Niagara-on-the-
Lake offered the *Nonsuch* honest hospitality, help and friendship.

The glow of Niagara-on-the-Lake was still bright and clear
when the *Nonsuch* reached Toronto on August 19 for her visit to the
Canadian National Exhibition. The CNE, "the largest annual
exhibition in the world," claims attendance figures in excess of three
million people each year, and this built-in audience made the fair a
mandatory stop for the *Nonsuch*. Everyone was confident that the
ship would be swamped with spectators during her two-week
engagement.

Fair officials had not needed persuasion to include the *Nonsuch* in the 1970 CNE. At the initial meeting with them early in the year, they had eagerly expressed their interest in the ship and agreed to provide publicity on her behalf; but a search for a berth convenient to the fair and satisfactory to the ship had continued until within a few weeks of her arrival. There had been moments when it seemed doubtful that anything suitable would be found. Various proposed sites had been dismissed because of shallow water, distance from the fair, or lack of protection from storms on the lake. A final investigation of the Lake Ontario shoreline in the vicinity of the exhibition grounds had produced a single possibility, at the south-eastern corner of Coronation Park, a five-minute walk from the fair. With no alternative and an obligation to the CNE which would be difficult to revoke at such a late date, the berth had been accepted, although it had several drawbacks: there were no electrical outlets, no fresh water supply, and the lake bottom was as uneven as the Rocky Mountains.

The appointed afternoon came, and just before arrival time, the *Nonsuch* could be seen through the mist of a cool drizzle that dampened the day and coated everything, from spirits to ships' hulls, with a drab, depressing grey. Her sails hung limp and lifeless as she motored through the flat water. Her cannons broke the silence, but they elicited little response from the handful of people who stood behind a rust-spotted chain link fence and watched as Captain Small manoeuvred the *Nonsuch* through the narrow gap in the breakwater and then alongside a littered, cement dock.

The arrival was carefully timed to avoid coinciding with the opening of the fair which annually captures premium attention in the press. Strategy suggested that competition be avoided by arriving two days before. The press, however, greeted the *Nonsuch* with total silence. Two weeks earlier the *Nonsuch* had come to Toronto for a one-day visit in conjunction with the opening of a new Company store. She had received lavish coverage and achieved the publicity milestone of the summer – prominent pictures of the *Nonsuch* against the backdrop of Toronto's impressive skyline in all three newspapers. Toronto had been generous to the *Nonsuch* that day, and it was naive to expect a duplicate response to her return; now she was old news in this sophisticated city.

Although CNE officials did everything in their power to promote the ship's presence, few people came. For the duration of the fair, the flat green surface of Coronation Park became a parking lot, and only the people who left their cars near the shore saw the *Nonsuch*. Fair visitors whose cars were near the entrance to the park could see little more than the upper portion of the mainmast. Few people were willing – or energetic enough – to leave the Exhibition's midway, cross six lanes of traffic on busy Lakeshore Boulevard, and then hike through a car-filled park to see a ship. It was asking too much.

Crew morale sagged. What a sorry contrast to Niagara-on-the-Lake! The crew had not seen so few people in any port that summer, and the inactivity made the days painfully long.

While the Toronto press ignored the return of the *Nonsuch* she unintentionally made the headlines the following week. Captain Small was obliged to vacate the CNE berth, as the ship kept touching the bottom. The CNE was advised of the change in location and the *Nonsuch* moved into Toronto Harbour at the foot of Bay Street.

The move caught the attention of the press, who quickly jumped on the item, taking the Exhibition and the Company by surprise. Newspaper and radio reports said the *Nonsuch* had been "removed" from the CNE because the Exhibition administrators had shown a lack of co-operation and had not publicized the vessel enough, and attributed these reasons to a Hudson's Bay Company representative. In both cases the reports were false, and in a letter to the president of the Exhibition regarding the controversy, the Company spokesman stated: "Low water at the berth necessitated the move. Between the time the *Nonsuch* arrived at the CNE, and her departure for her present berth inside Toronto Harbour, the water level off Coronation Park dropped approximately one foot and resulted in the ship resting on her keel. For the sheer safety of the ship, her Captain . . . had to look for another place to stay."

Moored at Coronation Park, Toronto, August 19, 1970

67

The Bay Street berth, however, had not been built to fill the needs of a touring seventeenth-century replica ketch; it was located a fair distance from the populated downtown area and the parking was poor. Most of those who saw the *Nonsuch* in Toronto Harbour came upon her by accident, not by design. It was impossible to publicize her new location effectively. People trickled to the docks, but crowds never came. Someone naively suggested to the Company that the *Nonsuch* would gain greater exposure if she was paraded through downtown Toronto and exhibited in Nathan Phillips Square opposite the City Hall – an exercise that would have taken months to arrange. She was not a contraption that could be taken apart, crated and assembled in an evening. The whole visit was a promotor's nightmare. The potential public relations triumph had backfired and become a disaster. There was nothing to do but leave, and on September 5 the *Nonsuch* slipped away. A gratifying weekend of activities at Port Credit restored the good humour of the ship and her crew.

The Company had not intended to operate the *Nonsuch* after 1970, but in spite of the debacle at the CNE, response to the ship had exceeded all expectation, and when construction of her museum home in Winnipeg was delayed, the Company decided to keep her in the Great Lakes for the next summer. The Lake Ontario shoreline had already been combed for a winter home for the *Nonsuch*. Ironically, of all the places investigated, only Canada's steel capital, Hamilton, had everything required for a wooden ship – namely a dock adjacent to a large storage shed that could double as a workshop.

By the time snow fell, the *Nonsuch* was flanked on three sides by empty shipping barrels to protect her from the weather. Jan Pearce and Sam Richards, retained for the winter, had erected a plastic-covered frame over the deck. The makeshift accommodations and the storage of many of her fascinating parts cost the *Nonsuch* much, if not all, of her nautical charm, and passersby who saw her at the foot of Catherine Street that winter may have wondered if she had been abandoned.

There was much to do that winter and spring in preparation for the summer ahead. The darkened, worn varnish and the chipped paint, those souvenirs of a season under sail, had to be erased from the masts, spars, cannons, carvings, the numerous pieces of iron-work and the hull above the waterline. Once stripped down, these surfaces were given fresh coats of the appropriate covering. The pine decks and the oak windlass were scraped, then oiled with linseed.

The 1971 Tour
The Great Lakes

Deck seams that required recaulking were filled with fresh oakum and then smeared with pitch to keep them watertight. The running rigging was replaced with Canadian hemp, and every inch of standing rigging was treated with tar. The sails were mended, and Captain Small sewed a topgallant sail which, when in use at the top of the mainmast, eliminated the slightly unfinished look the *Nonsuch* had had aloft.

Below the waterline, the hull was cleaned of green growth accumulated in the course of the ship's summer travels, then scraped, and finally given three coats of white paint: an undercoat, a topcoat and an application of anti-foulant paint. In April, after the ship had been returned by crane to the murky waters of Hamilton Harbour, a smaller crane was used to step the lower masts and bowsprit. The topmasts and the main topgallant were sent up by the crew using ropes. The ship was then rigged and loaded with gear.

This was typical preparatory work, a crew responsibility that had to be carried out at regular intervals to keep the ship in sailing trim. Although it was routine work with a fair share of dirt and discomfort, it was done carefully, with considerable love for the vessel and a desire – which required occasional reinforcement by the Captain – to have the *Nonsuch* look her best for those who would see her that year. The refit was begun by Jan Pearce and Sam Richards, whose services were supplemented in the spring when most of the crew were assembled. The work was accelerated by the return of former crew members Messrs. Rose-Taylor, Hunter, Epp, and Richard Quinn (who had been with the ship in the U.K.), and by the addition of newcomer Vicente Garcia Bisquert, an experienced

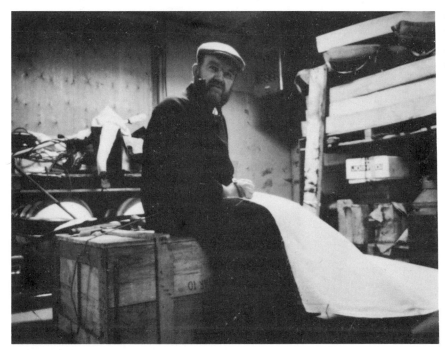

square-rig seaman from Denia, Spain. But as always seemed to be the case with *Nonsuch* refits, lack of time and unfavourable weather worked against the extra manpower, and the task was barely completed before the ship set off for the summer.

The ship's newest feature went unseen by most. It was her new toilet and holding tank, installed to adhere to the law of the twentieth century, not as a concession to the crew who were quite content with the ship's original pump-out plumbing. In July 1970, the Company had received a form letter from the Ontario Water Resources Commission saying the *Nonsuch* had been inspected by one of its men and found to be without the approved equipment. The Company had known of the anti-pollution measures governing Ontario waterways, but had only learned of them shortly before the ship was to leave Man and His World. An approved chemical toilet and holding tank had been obtained, but upon delivery it was obvious that several weeks work would be required to modify the cramped area below deck to accommodate this modern convenience. Consequently, the ship had operated throughout the summer with the equipment on board, but not installed.

By the time the *Nonsuch* departed from Hamilton to begin her 1971 tour, the new facilities were in operation, and the ship carried with her a list of pump-out stations located along the shores of the Great Lakes. This document was considered as essential to the ship and her crew as the navigational charts, but the men prepared themselves for a constipated summer, for most of the stations listed were inaccessibly situated in marinas designed for yachts with shallow drafts!

The Great Lakes were the ship's tour territory in 1971. She covered 2,320 miles, visiting communities between Toronto in the east to Duluth, Minnesota, at the western tip of Lake Superior, and was greeted with the same enthusiasm that had characterized her previous tours.

Like London, England, Montreal and Toronto, Chicago offered the little ketch the challenge of being noticed in a sophisticated, sprawling metropolis. She fared quite well, particularly with her noon-hour arrival on the narrow, skyscraper-lined Chicago River. The river is an urban canyon, a superb echo chamber that amplified magnificently the noise of the ship's 2½-pound cannons. Thousands came to the riverbanks or to balconies and windows high in the heavens to see, with astonishment, the small cause of the commotion.

An unscheduled stop for fuel and provisions at Kenosha, Wisconsin, brought a pleasant surprise, for it coincided with the official opening of a waterfront Holiday Inn, nautically decorated throughout. Scarcely had the last mooring rope been hitched, when the crew of the ketch were surrounded by curious and excited employees and guests who flooded the dock. Probably the person most profoundly affected by the arrival was the innkeeper, who, overjoyed at this unexpected climax to her festivities, made the crew guests of the house. Word of the ship's arrival spread quickly throughout Kenosha, and the local paper published notice of her presence. When she finally left early the next evening, it seemed to the men on deck that the entire town had assembled to watch.

With her passage through the Welland Canal, the shipping link between Lake Ontario and Lake Erie, the *Nonsuch* experienced the last major lock of the St. Lawrence Seaway system. The locks had been a great unknown facing her in 1970, and they continued to be a frightening experience for the crew. The massive gates and walls dwarfed the *Nonsuch*. At the bottom of an empty lock she looked like a tiny toy boat in an empty bathtub. Her miniature appearance was exaggerated when she shared a lock with a modern ship, like a goldfish and a whale in the same tank. Captain Small described the turbulence in the locks when the water was let in or out as being "like berthing under the foot of Niagara Falls."

Precautions were always taken to protect the ship from the lock's walls as she wobbled around in the strong currents, and at Welland the fenders were supplemented by the ship's rubber dinghy and the mattresses from the Captain's and the mate's berths.

While the 1971 tour had similarities to the ship's other seasons, it also had its contrasts. In Toronto, where she visited in June, she was no longer a dismal flop but a busy, popular attraction. When she returned to Niagara-on-the-Lake that same month, the welcoming multitude of 1970 was represented only by a few soggy fans on the dock to meet her, for the arrival neatly coincided with the end of a driving rainstorm. These two return engagements were indicative of the ship's 1971 season, for it was a summer tour opposite in many ways from the previous one.

The 1971 tour overcame the chief drawback of the past summer when the *Nonsuch* had whistle-stopped her way down the St. Lawrence and around the Canadian shore of Lake Ontario, visiting towns that were nearly neighbours. Often she had had to leave one community at sunrise in order to make an early evening arrival in another. The timetable was so stringent that the ship's auxiliary engine, referred to by the crew as the "iron topsail," was used frequently.

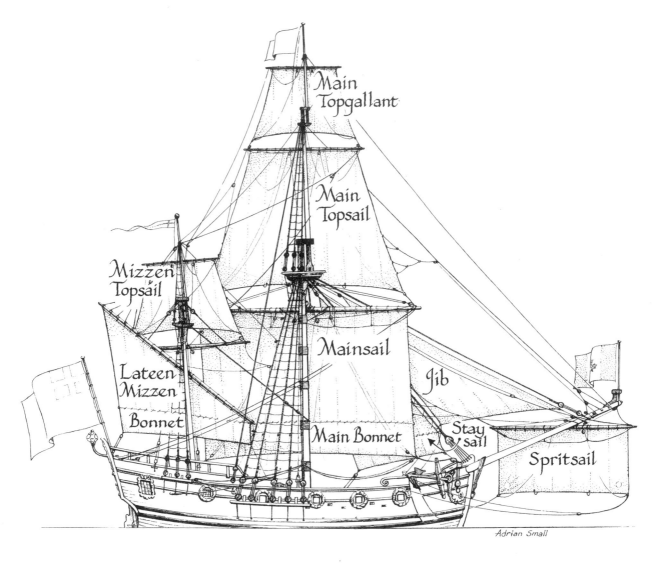

Main
Topgallant

Main
Topsail

Mizzen
Topsail

Mainsail

Jib

Lateen
Mizzen

Bonnet

Main Bonnet

Stay
sail

Spritsail

Adrian Small

The sail plan of the *Nonsuch*

Chicago skyscrapers
tower above the
Nonsuch

On the Great Lakes, however, this changed. The selected ports of call were miles apart. In contrast to last year's seven-mile motor trip from Williamstown, Ontario to Cornwall, in 1971 the *Nonsuch* travelled approximately 462 miles between Chicago and Sault Ste. Marie. The ship sailed most of the 230 miles between Beaver Island, Michigan, and Kenosha, and did so in less than forty-eight hours. The crew were delighted to exchange the confining St. Lawrence with its strong current for the vast spaces of the Great Lakes, where stiff breezes and long distances between ports made it possible to sail the *Nonsuch* as she should be sailed.

Ironically, after such impressive accomplishments on the Lakes, the *Nonsuch* finished the summer rather ingloriously. In a flat calm on Lake Superior off Two Harbours, Minnesota, her engine seized and in order to cover the remaining twenty-three miles and arrive at Duluth as scheduled, the mate engaged the services of the *Edna G.,* built in 1896, the last active steam tug on the upper Great Lakes. She brought the becalmed ketch to near the entrance of the Duluth ship canal, where the towline was transferred to a coast-guard lifeboat for the short haul to the dock.

Whether at the end of a towline, or stuck in the harbour at Thunder Bay on her only major grounding of the season, or without her captain who was absent some of the summer with an ulcerated varicose vein, the *Nonsuch* in 1971 was a ship whose operation had been greatly improved. Captain and crew worked together more smoothly with a year's shared experience behind them. Morale improved when the stifling period costumes were sent into semi-retirement, and replaced (except for official arrivals) by blue cotton smocks and white duck trousers. The tour planners had become acquainted with their charge; they had learned to gauge her manoeuverability, speed and behaviour in locks, and could plan her movements accordingly. With the experience of the past season it was much easier to forecast public and press response to the ship and to determine effective ways to improve her public relations.

The public had not been admitted to the ship when she was in the U.K., except when she was not officially on view or when the public were not at the quayside. Experience in 1970 proved that there was usually no time – except in the early hours of the morning – when the *Nonsuch* was not in the public eye. Even pouring rain on the day after she arrived in Gananoque, Ontario, did not keep the droves of people away, and it was not uncommon for the crew to have to eject intruders who jumped on board long after midnight.

Initially, the Company had adopted the U.K. approach to the public and carefully stated in its printed material on the *Nonsuch* and to the press that it was "not planned" to allow the public on board because of the limited space above and below deck, but that members of the crew would be available on most occasions to answer questions. Visits on board the ship would be limited to official parties and invited guests.

Fortunately, the Company did not take a rigid stance, for the Canadian public found this restricting policy completely unacceptable – as did the Captain, who had always been in favour of opening the ship, even when she was in the U.K. The crew were besieged by requests for permission to go on board. The reply that the ship was too small to accommodate the public was met with obvious displeasure, much disappointment and the often-heard remark, "What is the point of bringing the ship here if the public is not admitted?"

As a change in policy was obviously necessary, official public hours had finally been introduced in 1970, eliminating the main source of public criticism of the *Nonsuch*. But in 1971 public hours were standardized for each port; they were given to the press in advance of the ship's visit and displayed on the *Nonsuch* by means of a clearly visible sign. As always, there was no charge to come on board.

Another new feature in 1971 was the use of the ship for cruises, something for which she was not ideally constituted. She always carried extra life-jackets, but technically she carried only enough life-saving equipment, as specified by the British Board of Trade, to accommodate "10 persons and no more." Her decks were narrow, slippery when wet, and clogged with rope, gun carriages and cannons. When she was sailing, the congestion on deck was often increased, as her rubber fenders, her boat and sometimes her gangway were piled on board. The men had to be free to move quickly upon command, and while they soon memorized the position of permanent obstacles, there was always the danger of collision with guests and possible injury. Furthermore the galley and the plumbing were scarcely adequate for the needs of the crew, let alone passengers. Nevertheless, it had not been unusual for guests to be on board when the ship was sailing both in England and in Canada, and in the summer of 1971 the Company expanded the practice to include official cruises for selected groups of people.

The testing ground for this scheme was Toronto in June. This time the *Nonsuch* shunned Toronto Harbour and her infamous CNE berth in favour of a dock at Ontario Place, a multi-million dollar waterfront attraction on man-made islands. The former static program of having the ship arrive and remain at dockside throughout her stay was replaced with an experimental program of activities: for a few hours, Warner Brothers Records used the ship to promote its Nonesuch label; she was open to the public every evening and afternoons on weekends; Captain Small appeared on a national television talk show; the Company held a children's colouring contest and the sixteen winners, were taken on a sail around Toronto harbour. The *Nonsuch* sailed for members of the Big Brothers Association of Metropolitan Toronto and took members of the Eaton family, who own one of the Company's major retail competitors, for an afternoon cruise.

The cruise was the most rewarding ingredient in the experimental program. It was the ideal way to thank the volunteers in each port who had helped to arrange the ship's visit or to introduce the media to the ship. What a tremendous thrill for a youngster to win a sail on the ship, to cruise around his home-town harbour taking a turn at the tiller! And besides, a cruise kept the crew sailing, albeit in a somewhat limited fashion, which is what they enjoyed most. From a modest Toronto beginning, the cruise became the ship's most effective public relations vehicle.

Nonsuch Ketch — Pt. Weller towards Pt. Colborne

Monday 28 June 1971 — Welland Canal

	Cours	Winds	Baro.	Temp.	
0500	~ Courses as required in Seaway Welland Canal ~				Call all hands on deck. 1st Lock opening.
0515		Calm 1st Lock.			Cast off under power. Lord Mayor Fred. Goring, his wife, the Lady Mayoress, and family arrive at the quay to bid us farewell ~ a very friendly gesture at this early hour. They could hardly have spent 4 hrs in their beds. We leave them standing on the quay in the darkness and lock into first lock.
0545					Clear the lock with some difficulty caused by turbulence.
0605		2nd Lock.			Enter and secure in the second lock ~ port side to for all locks.
0620					Lock open but delayed by downbound traffic. The Ketch is well prepared to traverse the locks alone; all yards a-cockbill, port anchor hoisted inboard, the Rubber Boat secured outboard to the main shrouds & channel, all fenders in use, port side light bracket unshipped ~ portable V.H.F. radio on deck.
0635					Clear of second lock and proceed southwards.
0645					S/S "Fort York", Laker, passes downbound.
0650					Pass under Garden City Skyline Bridge.
0705					Make fast to tie-up wall below lock 3.
0715		3rd Lock.			Enter lock 3 and secure port side to. All well so far.
0740					Clear the lock and proceed.
0755					Make fast to tie-up wall below lock 4. Await D/B vessel.
0835		4th Lock.			Enter lock 4 and make fast. This is the first of the "Flight locks" of which I had been warned. With this lock empty and the next full, there is a double head of water ~ over 60ft. ~ which will flow into this lock when the gates close astern. The cabin mattresses (Capt. and mate's) are got out and secured, one to the mizzen channels and the other to the port cat-head. The lock is filled rapidly and hands fend off aft ~ no great difficulty but the mattresses suffer.
0900		5th Lock.			Enter flight lock 5 ~ no problems.
0930		6th "			Shift into lock 6 ~ Burst the Rubber Boat and one of the fenders but no serious difficulties.
0950					Clear lock and shift to tie-up wall below lock 7. Awaiting downbound laker.
1045		7th Lock.			Enter lock 7 and secure.
1115					Cleared the lock, no difficulties.
1120					The Halco laker "Frakcliffe Hall" passes downbound.
1130					Guard Gate passed.
1135					The laker S/S "Mantadoc" passes downbound.
1145	Alongside at Beaver Dock.				Secured alongside the Beaver Board dock having negotiated the last of the difficult locks without too much trouble. Being well ahead of time we can afford to wait here and square up the ship before Welland.
Noon		SSE 1	1014	75°	Cloudy & fine wr. with little or no wind. Becoming v. hot.

45			Square the yards. Stow rubber boat on board.
15			Fished the port anchor and made all ship-shape in
30			general. Hands to dinner
			Cast off under power and proceed towards Welland.
			Very hot weather. The pitch is melting and running
345			in the deck seams. Wash down decks.
			Starb'd. watch relieved, port watch take the deck.
00			Resecure the port lamp bracket to the shrouds.
045			Loose and set all plain sail — calm — continue under
			power. Passing under Bridge Nº 13 and approaching
			the berth at Welland. Laker s/s "Piginou Bay" passes l/b.
			Fire 5-gun salute to the town.
20			Secure alongside the quay on the canal at Welland, on
			South side of Bridge 14 port side to. Gangway landed
			from the quarterdeck rail
30			With the Canadian Sea Cadet Corps "Bellorophon"
	Alongside at Welland		manning the gangway, the Mayor of Welland and
			guests are welcomed on board. The weather is too
		Temperature on Deck has reached 90° this day.	hot and stifling for the guests to remain long in the
			cabin and shortly leave for the town accompanied
45			by the Captain and the port watch. Mr. Hamilton,
			manager of the Hudson's Bay Store here, acts as host.
00			Richard Quinn, Cook, ashore briefly, to purchase provisions.
	6		Captain and port watch return on board, exhausted.
920			Stand by for clearance from the Seaway to proceed.
			Extend my thanks to Lt. Peacock of the R.C.S.C. Corps
			for standing by all afternoon in uncomfortably hot
			weather. Cast off and proceed under power
			Fire two-gun salute for the R.C.S.C. "Belorophon"
			and pass under bridges 15 and 16.
945			Pass under bridge Nº 17. Brace sharp up the main
			and spritsail yards in readiness for the last lock.
000	Calm 1015	79°	Calm, hot and clear weather
20	8th Lock.		Enter lock Nº 8 and make fast port side to.
30			Clear out of lock. Proceed to Port Colborne
			looking for a quiet berth for the night.
52			Secure alongside to the town quay at Pt. Colborne
	Port Colborne		above Bridge Nº 21 starb'd. side to. Secure fore & aft.
30			Hands to swim over the side.
00			Supper. Night watch set. Shore leave granted.
300	Calm		All hands on board. Secure for the night.
			And so ends a long, hard and tiring day. I had
	Distance Sailed:		intended to continue on passage out into Lake Erie
	Pt. Weller — Pt. Colborne		tonight but all hands will be better off with
	≈ 23		a full night's sleep and ready for an early start
	Previous ~~214~~ 223		tomorrow
	Total = ~~237~~ 246		Gunners Report ~ At 1445 under bridge 13 appr. Welland
			5 guns fired, nos. 2 & 4 double charged. At 1920 Fire 2 guns
			leaving Welland. Charges remaining: 6. Guns fired: 7
			Total guns fired = 94.

The *Nonsuch* was so popular at Ontario Place that the Company was reluctant to end her sailing career. Since construction of her museum home had been delayed again, there was nothing to prevent another season under sail, and the Company began to think about British Columbia: The Pacific slope was rich in Hudson's Bay Company history; there was that magnificent scenery – could there be a more complimentary setting for their unique ship? British Columbia was one of the Company's most important retail markets; and how appropriate it would be, for the *Nonsuch* to have salt water against her hull one more time before she retired to museum life! The idea took shape, and with a swashbuckling spirit reminiscent of the Hudson's Bay Company's fur trading days, the Company proposed that the *Nonsuch* sail to British Columbia.

Overland to the Pacific

When the Company approached Captain Small with the plan, he was enthusiastic and felt certain that the crew would feel the same. He was delighted at the prospect of silencing those who had scoffed at the way the *Nonsuch* had crossed the Atlantic, and he outlined a plan for the voyage: the ship would sail from Duluth, Minnesota, across the Great Lakes to Oswego, New York, down the Hudson River system to the Atlantic, around the rim of North America through the Panama Canal, and finally to Vancouver, British Columbia. Captain Small estimated that the journey would cover 7,436 miles in ten months.

The crew was not informed of the voyage until eight weeks later during the ship's visit to Thunder Bay. At a meeting of ship's personnel, a Company representative delivered a carefully prepared speech, telling the crew how successful the 1971 tour had been and how appreciative the Company was of their efforts. The speech came to a climax with the announcement of a fourth season for the *Nonsuch* and the proposal to sail her to the west coast, operate her for the summer of 1972 and then bring her overland to Winnipeg.

There was absolute silence. The crew sat motionless, their faces empty of response. The quiet was broken only when the Company representative specifically asked for their comments.

The men were pleased to learn of the fourth season and eager to sign on the ship again – for the summer. But they were tired after another demanding tour and were looking forward to its completion in a few weeks. They had not a remote interest in weighing anchor in Duluth and sailing for nearly a year in order to deliver the ship to British Columbia for the following summer. Furthermore, Philip Rose-Taylor and Jan Pearce refused to sail the *Nonsuch* on the open sea, on the grounds of her questionable stability, in spite of the fact that she had survived severe gales in both English and Canadian waters.

This was reasoned opposition, but no one in that room wanted to lose the chance of a season on the Canadian west coast. For the next two hours alternative means of getting the *Nonsuch* from Thunder Bay to Vancouver were thrashed out. In the end, the group reached the unanimous decision to recommend to the Company that the vessel be taken overland to the Pacific – a prospect which the Captain had once described as "too dismal to contemplate." Pearce thought that this would require some alterations to the hull, but would not involve the removal of anything that could not be replaced with time and labour – and money. The Company accepted the recommendation the following week.

The Company had always known that at some stage the *Nonsuch* would have to travel on land to reach Winnipeg, probably from the western end of Lake Superior. Railway transportation had been ruled out; the ship's dimensions exceeded the maximum allowed. Commercial trucking firms had expressed a clear disinterest. The only company that had been willing and confident they could do the job was Riverton Boatworks Ltd. The firm, located in Riverton, Manitoba, north of Winnipeg, had a growing sideline of hauling boats over various portions of North America.

Early in 1968, the Company had asked Riverton's president Mr. Chris Thorsteinson, to plot a course for the *Nonsuch* from Lake Superior to Winnipeg, which he had done. In June 1971 when the plan to sail the ship to Vancouver was a possibility, the Company had asked Mr. Thorsteinson if it was possible to bring by road from Vancouver to Winnipeg. After two weeks of travelling the highways in the northern United States from Minnesota to Washington and the
82

Trans-Canada system from Vancouver to Winnipeg, he had reported that a route appeared open. He suggested the use of a combination of roads on both sides of the border, since the Canadian Rockies would be impassable to the *Nonsuch*.

Two months later, following the silent summit meeting with the crew in Thunder Bay and the consequent change of plan, it appeared that the Company had approached the overland route backwards, and the scheme was reversed. The *Nonsuch*, instead of going overland west to east, would do the exact opposite, and it was Riverton's view that if the ship could complete the trip they had charted in one direction, she could do so in the other.

On September 2, after completing the official summer tour, Captain Small took the *Nonsuch* across Duluth Harbour to Fraser Shipyard Inc., in Superior, Wisconsin, for the enormous task of converting her to a roadworthy amphibian. The bowsprit and all the rigging, masts, yards and sails were removed, as they had been at the end of other seasons; but this time almost everything removable was taken out as well, in order to reduce the weight of the hull and shave precious inches off its dimensions. Out came the galley equipment, the toilet and holding tank, the two 80-gallon water tanks, all the floor boards (which were "too damaged to be of further use") and the sixty-nine lead pigs used for ballast. The windlass was unloaded and the rudder removed. A small crane was used to extract the ship's engine and the 200-gallon fuel tank. By September 7 all of the gear except the bowsprit and lowermasts had been crated and stored in a van. Night watches were discontinued on the *Nonsuch*, for as the Captain remarked, there was "nothing that can be removed from the ship – unless it be the ship herself."

The Riverton crew, with the help of Jan Pearce, began to modify the exterior of the hull. They removed the port and starboard channels, catheads, chain plates and deadeyes, the carving at the starboard quarter and the two gunport wreaths at midships on the port side. A heavy lift crane then raised the hull from the lake and rested it on four wooden keel-blocks that were built up approximately three feet to make working space underneath. The ship was shored up with massive timbers jammed under the gunport rims, and

83

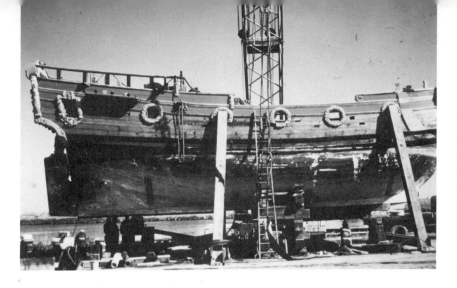

Minus masts, spars and rigging, stripped of equipment, lead keel and most of her external projections, the *Nonsuch* is carefully lowered onto her starboard side and bolted to a cradle for the overland journey to Seattle

the men began the laborious task of removing the eighteen tons of lead from the ship's keel.

When this was completed a final job remained. "There was doubt in the minds of Fraser's management about putting the ship on her side," wrote the Captain, "but Mr. Thorsteinson knew what he was doing . . . ." Using a crane and a wire sling which passed under the keel and around the vessel at midships, the hull was rolled gently onto its starboard side and bolted to a custom-built iron cradle. The aft cabin and the chart room did not fare very well, for the bolts damaged much of the panelling on the starboard side. The cradle rested on sets of wheels toward the ship's stern. A curved bar, like a goose neck, followed the lines of the bow and connected the cradle to a truck cab. On its side the hull measured 53 feet in length and 20 feet across at the stern. It was a scant 6 inches off the ground, giving it an overall height of 16 feet 6 inches, but this could be reduced by about 4 inches by repositioning the gooseneck on the truck cab. The conversion was tested and modified. The transformation was complete; in forty days a charming period ketch had become her own flat-bed trailer. A short test drive around the yard confirmed that the *Nonsuch* was ready to roll west.

84

While the *Nonsuch* was undergoing her metamorphosis at
Fraser's Shipyard, representatives of the Hudson's Bay Company
were searching for a shipyard in Vancouver that had the skills and
services to help with the reassembly of the ship, one that was
accessible by road. With the help of Captain Barney Johnson, retired
harbour-master of the port of Vancouver, a satisfactory yard was
found in North Vancouver. To be certain that the *Nonsuch* could be
driven to the door, the Company's representatives investigated the
highways from the U.S. border around Blaine, Washington, north to
Vancouver. There were several low bridges that looked doubtful,
and an inquiry to the provincial highway department confirmed the
Company's fears. The department would not grant them a permit to
bring the *Nonsuch* to Vancouver by road: she was too tall.

A week's work had been wasted. Stunned but not defeated, the
Company shifted its search to south of the international boundary,
with the objective of rerouting the *Nonsuch* to a shipyard in
Washington state, or bringing her north to Vancouver on a barge.
For the next two weeks, a small band of people dedicated them-
selves to solving the singular migration problem facing the
Nonsuch. There were Captain Small and his wife (who had recently

joined him from England), Captain A.F. Raynaud and Captain Harold Huycke, friends of Captain Small's who lived in the Seattle area, Captain Johnson from Vancouver, Chris Thorsteinson and a representative of the Hudson's Bay Company.

It was a frustrating fortnight. After several long, unrewarding days the weary searchers were tempted to cancel the whole plan to bring the ship west. The days sped by. Valuable time was wasted waiting to see people, asking directions – and then getting lost – waiting for people to return telephone calls, driving miles from one place to another to investigate a lead, a prospect, a slender thread of a solution. Ports on Puget Sound north of Seattle were explored. The Captain and his search party devoted days to Seattle itself, visiting shipyards and possible launching points. In the city's office of the U.S. Army Corps of Engineers, Captain Small spent a full afternoon – interrupted briefly by an unexpected firedrill which evacuated the building – on long-distance telephone calls (courtesy of the U.S. taxpayer), discussing with the Corps Walla Walla District Office the feasibility of floating the *Nonsuch* in the Columbia River at Pasco, Washington, and then on to Seattle by water.

The entire west-to-east route from Seattle to Lethbridge, Alberta, was travelled to review the ship's itinerary with state highway departments and secure permission to cross their territory. Notes on overpasses en route were started but stopped because of their questionable value: the *Nonsuch* would be travelling in the opposite direction! The excursion made it clear, however, that Montana should present no problems, that Idaho would not be too difficult, but that the state of Washington would be as much of a challenge as virgin North America must have been to its first explorers.

In Washington, the *Nonsuch* would be restricted to four-lane divided state roads. If necessary she could use county or city roads, provided the appropriate authorities approved. Members of the search party drove along Interstate 90, the ship's designated channel between Spokane and Seattle, from east to west. They listed most of the bridges encountered and noted the presence or absence of exit roads serving each one. They attempted to determine the height of each overpass, either by asking local officials or by finding it on the list of bridges supplied by the state highway department. In an extreme situation, Captain Small ventured forth courageously into the middle of a frantic Seattle freeway carrying a pole, to produce the measurement personally. Six detours lay in the ship's path between Spokane and Seattle; each was driven and documented for future reference; approval to use city or county roads was obtained.

During this fourteen-day flurry of activity, the Company decided to keep the *Nonsuch* in Seattle for the winter at the Marco Marine Construction and Design Company yard on Lake Union, a shipyard that could answer all of the ketch's unique needs. Captain Huycke, who worked for the Puget Sound Tug and Barge Company in Seattle, suggested that the *Nonsuch* be driven to that Company's property on the Duwamish River, where she could easily be launched and towed to the Marco Yard. It was an excellent plan, but it raised the problem of finding a route for the *Nonsuch* through the nightmarish network of Seattle's freeways. This final puzzle stymied the searchers for several days until they made contact with Frank Shaughnessy of Shaughnessy & Company Inc., a firm with the intriguing reputation of moving the most stationary of objects. Mr. Shaughnessy knew how to get the *Nonsuch* to the Duwamish.

On October 13, in the cold darkness of 1:30 a.m., the *Nonsuch* left Superior, Wisconsin. Jan Pearce and Philip Rose-Taylor travelled with her, offering navigational help to her overland helmsman from Riverton Boatworks. The state of Minnesota restricted her travels to between 1:00 and 5:00 a.m., whereas everywhere else she was required to move during the daylight hours, when she would be less of a hazard to users of the same road. She was escorted by pilot cars in front and behind. The hull was decorated, although not enhanced, by flashing amber lights and red flags. The deck side of the hull was wrapped in a banner proclaiming NONSUCH HUDSON'S BAY COMPANY DULUTH TO VANCOUVER. By the time the *Nonsuch* left the Fraser yard the information on the sign

**In downtown Portage
la Prairie, Manitoba**

**Passing autumn
wheatfields near Gren-
fell, Saskatchewan**

was obsolete; by the time the she reached Winnipeg two days later, the banner had been torn beyond repair.

It was a conspicuous caravan, one of the strangest sights passing motorists would ever see on the road. From Superior, the *Nonsuch* travelled north-west across Minnesota to Warroad, and entered Canada at 4:30 a.m. on October 15 through Sprague, Manitoba. When the sun rose two hours later, progress resumed. The ship continued in the same direction through Steinbach to the Trans-Canada Highway, then west to Winnipeg and Assiniboia Downs where the ship remained until October 20. Despite the driving rain that fell during those five days, Riverton's men added another axle to the cradle under the *Nonsuch* to comply with Washington State regulations, and the words NONSUCH HUDSON'S BAY COMPANY DULUTH TO SEATTLE were painted in bold black letters on the white undersides of the ship.

**Among Montana
mountains en route
to Helena**

**Reaching the summit of
Lookout Pass with the
help of a road grader**

With structural and artistic work complete, the *Nonsuch*
resumed her journey west, now in the company of the trailer with
her masts and keel. (The van with the gear travelled independently
to the coast.) Her route followed the Trans-Canada Highway
through the centre of Portage la Prairie and north of Brandon,
Manitoba, into Saskatchewan where she rolled past mile after mile
of golden wheat fields. At Medicine Hat, Alberta, she left the
Trans-Canada for Lethbridge, where she arrived on October 25
after a twelve-hour journey of 245 miles covered at an average
speed of 20 m.p.h..

The *Nonsuch* had smooth sailing across Montana until she
reached Saltese, a tiny spit of a town at the base of Lookout Pass
4,763 feet above sea level, the boundary between Montana and
Idaho. The highway through the pass was under construction and
highway officials refused to allow the *Nonsuch* to use the detour

because of the unsettled weather and the fear that she might founder and block the route. They requested that she remain in Saltese until the new road was more passable. The *Nonsuch* was therefore temporarily abandoned in the town and the Riverton team returned to Manitoba while Philip Rose-Taylor and Jan Pearce continued to Seattle to arrange lodgings for the winter.

When everyone returned to Saltese on November 15, the road that had caused the twelve-day delay was still only dirt and gravel; nevertheless permission to travel on it was granted and the *Nonsuch* started up the mountain. Chains had been attached to the wheels under the ship but she was soon stuck in the soft surface. To reach the summit and the State of Idaho, the *Nonsuch* had to be hauled over the rest of Lookout Pass – in a snowstorm – by a road grader.

The *Nonsuch* cavalcade found its way through Spokane, Washington, on the morning of November 17, following a twisted course along side roads, residential streets and main thoroughfares. It was one of the most complex detours she had had to make, but miraculously, it was an easy passage. Fresh from this minor triumph, however, she struck a bridge over the freeway four miles west of the city. There was no way around this obstacle; she had to go under or she would not reach Seattle. It was much lower than the overpass she had encountered south of Winnipeg, where she had been easily extricated by repositioning the gooseneck on the truck cab. More ingenuity was needed now. The hull was lowered, but it remained a fraction too high. The resourceful Riverton crew let the air out of all the tires under the hull, and greased the gunnel amid-ships on top. The truck inched forward; the hull screeched loudly as it scraped under the bridge until, at last, it reached freedom on the other side.

Six weeks after leaving Superior, Wisconsin, the *Nonsuch,* safe and intact although spattered by mud and weather, reached the Puget Sound Tug and Barge Company after travelling over two thousand miles of road. Captain Raynaud inspected the vessel for the Company and found her to be in good condition, with damage limited to "raking, gouging, and scuffing on the port side of the hull, approximately in the midship section." He noted in his report that one carved figure had been "decapitated"; the face of this mermaid had fallen off (but was saved) in Superior. London would have blushed to learn that it had been fastened only with glue.

A crane, slings and tires were assembled the next morning. All the ship's bolts were "backed out and burned off, and all other interferences removed." The crane lifted the ship from the cradle and Jan Pearce installed wooden plugs in the bolt holes. After a short rest on a bed of tires, the *Nonsuch* was raised on her keel, shifted to the edge of the dock and lowered into the Duwamish. The tug *Goliah* led her to the Marco yard.

In the ship's Log for November 24, 1971, Jan Pearce, with classic understatement, entered, "And so ends a very interesting project. Now comes the time-consuming task of reassembly." And in a letter Captain Small wrote, "It was yet another episode in the strange life of a small ketch. I am quite sure this second *Nonsuch* has had a more adventuresome life than her predecessor. I wonder what is in store for her next?"

The mammoth task of connecting the hundreds of loose *Nonsuch* parts delivered to Seattle was tackled almost immediately by Jan Pearce and Philip Rose-Taylor. Captain Small returned home to Brixham for the winter, but he was back in Seattle by mid-March. A month later he had assembled a crew of six which included Messrs. Rose-Taylor, Pearce, Richards, Weatherill, Quinn and new-comer Thomas Stevens from Aldeburgh, England. Two Seattle students, Jim Meckley and John Janus, were subsequently hired to sail with the ship for the summer. This was still insufficient manpower to complete work on the ship by the early May deadline established by the Company, and a damp April frequently inter-rupted progress. As the crew was pressed for time, the Company authorized Captain Small to hire the Marco yard for a variety of jobs that did not require a specialized knowledge of the ship.

The 1972 Tour

Puget Sound and British Columbia Waters

Because of the number of indirect expenditures involved, the exact cost of transporting and refitting the *Nonsuch* will never be determined, but those expenses directly connected with the project exceeded $90,000. This staggering sum was far more than the Company had ever anticipated. But it had been a unique undertak-ing; there was no guidance from past experience, and there had been unexpected and costly complications. The overland journey had taken much longer than expected, with the result that Riverton's $14,500 estimate soared beyond $50,000. In the drive to have the *Nonsuch* ready for commitments in early May, it was essential to hire the Marco yard to scrape, paint and revarnish the hull and caulk the decks seams, but at $11.50 per hour per man it was expensive. Bills came regularly from a number of sources. The Company had no choice, however – unless it decided to abandon the tour – but to wince, swallow and send cheques in return.

On May 6, the *Nonsuch* was officially introduced to the Seattle citizenry when she participated in a parade on the Opening Day of the Pacific North-West yachting season. Mr. J.L. Williams, commo-dore of the Seattle Yacht Club which hosted the annual event, wrote to the Company describing it. "Participating in our ceremony and parade are some thirty-five yachting organizations and 2,500 boats of

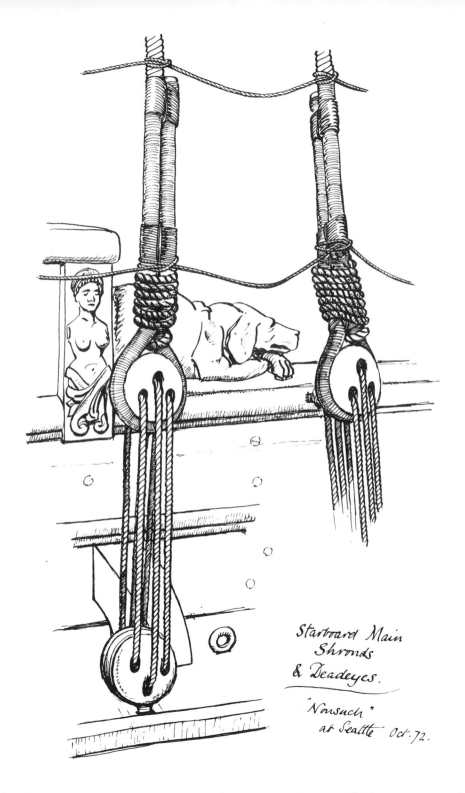

Starboard Main
Shrouds
& Deadeyes.

"Nonsuch"
at Seattle Oct. 72.

all sizes, shapes and description. This year, as always, the record was broken in terms of numbers. In addition we had a dozen live steam boats in parade with their attendant smoke, colour and fabulous whistles.

"But the outstanding participant of all was the appearance of your ketch, *Nonsuch* under full sail through the narrow cut and passing in review. Her six-gun salute brought cheers from the estimated 40,000 people on shore and the thousand boats lining the parade route. Never before have we had the honor of such a distinguished vessel in parade on Opening Day."

It was an event equally memorable for the *Nonsuch* and her crew. She was one of an unbelievable collection of floating craft and objects sandwiched into tiny Portage Bay, the assembly point for the parade. There were luxury launches and lifeboats, powerboats and canoes, tugs, trawlers, the steamboats, and an assortment of unusual vessels including a motorized bathtub, a reasonably accurate replica of an Eskimo kayak, a powered raft and pedalboats. All of them were making as much noise as possible with whatever was at their disposal: whistles, bells, sirens, floating choirs and quartets, horns, radios and engines all contributed to the unmelodic din. The *Nonsuch* could have punctuated the score with her cannons, but firing them in such close quarters would surely have shattered something.

On signal, the participants were to proceed in turn through the Montlake Cut, a narrow, grassy-banked link to Lake Washington, and form review lines facing one another through which each vessel would pass. The parade would have been more of a spectacle if there had been sunshine and wind, but neither were present, and like all the captains that day, Captain Small was prepared to motor his ship into Lake Washington. Then a remarkable thing happened. Only minutes before the *Nonsuch* was to perform, a breeze began to blow, not just a transitory puff or a muscular head wind, but a breeze tailor-made in strength and direction to enable the *Nonsuch* to pass in review using all but her spritsail.

The *Nonsuch* spent the summer sailing in Puget Sound and

95

**At Shilshole Bay
Marina, Seattle,
May 1972**

British Columbia waters. She criss-crossed the international border several times, dividing her time almost equally between Canada and the United States. While in American waters she visited the San Juan Islands which lie between Vancouver Island and mainland Washington. That year the San Juans celebrated their 100th anniversary as part of the U.S., an association which was preceded by a curious piece of history involving the Hudson's Bay Company.

In the 1850's this picturesque chain of islands was the centre of a dispute between Britain and the U.S. concerning the international boundary between Vancouver Island and continental U.S. Although the boundary question had been partially settled in 1846 by the Oregon Treaty, the status of the San Juan Islands remained uncertain. From 1853 to 1859 various disputes erupted on San Juan between the Hudson's Bay Company and a handful of American citizens, all of whom had property claims on the island. The situation reached an absurd climax in 1859 when one of the American settlers shot and killed a Hudson's Bay officer's hog, which was rooting in his garden. The latent antagonism flared up, and British and American military reinforcements were sent to the island. But the "Pig War" was over as soon as it had begun, and the Treaty of Washington settled the boundary question in 1872 by placing the San Juan archipelago under the jurisdiction of the United States.

Canadians, particularly those in the employ of the Hudson's Bay Company, were always curious about the reaction of Americans to the *Nonsuch*. Except for a Chicago lady who launched legal proceedings against the Company, claiming undefined personal injury through negligent operation of the ship, Americans adored the *Nonsuch,* and she had experienced an excellent reception at American ports in previous summers. But in every way, the American response in 1972 was unprecedented. With little prompting, and minimal expenditure by the Company, people thronged to see the ship. Heavy crowds and long line-ups swamped her at Seattle's Shilshole Bay and necessitated extra control measures. The floating pontoon she used at the Everett Yacht Club in Washington almost sank because of the number of people on it, and consequently the ship had to be moved to a more substantial pier.

97

The Company devoted considerably more time and money to organizing and promoting the *Nonsuch* in British Columbia waters than it did in Puget Sound. This was particularly true in Victoria and Vancouver, where the Company advertised her presence and developed elaborate programs using the ship. These extra efforts were rewarding, but they did not produce appreciably greater results than the ship achieved in Puget Sound virtually on her own. Her weekend visit to Tacoma, her southernmost port of the summer, was organized completely by mail and no more than six long-distance telephone calls. The dock she used had been selected sight unseen but it proved to be one of the best of the season. This minimal organizational effort produced throngs surpassing any the *Nonsuch* had seen since Niagara-on-the-Lake.

In contrast, the Company spent months combing the Vancouver waterfront from Kitsilano to the Centennial Docks in search of a suitable berth, and found only one that barely met the ship's peculiar needs. In view of the amount of work and expenditure, it was surprising that the *Nonsuch* was not inundated with visitors. Still, in Victoria and Vancouver and all along the coast, whether she made a scheduled or an unscheduled stop, people did come by the hundreds to see her, and they loved what they saw.

In a fresh wind on Puget Sound, approaching the Everett Yacht Club

Her decks crowded with guests, the *Nonsuch* was an added attraction in the 1972 Swiftsure Race, run annually from Victoria, B.C. to Cape Flattery, Washington

Except, perhaps for one member of Vancouver's Kitsilano yacht club, who cursed the ship when he was startled by the discharge of one of her cannons and injured his head on the fittings of his foredeck.

British Columbians opened their hearts and their homes to the ship with a generosity that was described in a letter from crewman Alfred Weatherill:

The cruise of the *Nonsuch* in British Columbia waters was by any standard a highlight in our lives and one which will not easily slip from our memory. The many kindnesses showered on us was overwhelming to the point of embarrassment . . . Such as the fishermen who quietly placed several salmon on the deck and departed unobserved so that we were unable to thank them. I must say 'thank you' also to the man who hired a suite of rooms at a hotel so that we could shower and enjoy a few hours of 'soft' living, and who we were unable to contact before we left his remote town. There were many others, too, who offered us the facilities of their bathrooms, loaned us cars so that we could explore the neighbourhood, took us into their homes and wined and dined us . . . The woman who hastily baked four to five dozen cookies when we briefly stopped by her out-of-the way corner of Vancouver Island . . . A personal memory of a few quiet hours one evening spent listening to gramaphone records at the invitation of a couple who had earlier visited the ship . . .

In spite of the organizational extremes the Company went to in Victoria and Vancouver, slick organization did not characterize the ship's tour in British Columbia. An administrative blunder resulted in the simultaneous arrival of two groups of about fifteen people for a cruise around Horseshoe Bay. Captain Small, not wanting to disappoint his guests, found room for them all on a cramped but pleasant cruise.

Through an internal misunderstanding, the tour organizers forgot to inform the town of Ladysmith on Vancouver Island of the ship's visit, and a stinging editorial entitled "How Not to Draw A Crowd" appeared in the *Ladysmith-Chemainus Chronicle* after her departure. "We don't know how much money the Hudson's Bay Company spent on building its beautiful replica of the *Nonsuch*," said the paper, "or how much it cost to ship it out to the west coast, but we assume the expenditure was made in the interest of public

Close hauled on the starboard tack in Howe Sound

100

relations. It certainly was an imaginative way to draw attention to the fact that the Company has now been doing business in Canada for more than 300 years. Because of the excellent job the Company has done in recreating the historic vessel and the many points it has visited since its arrival in Canada, we hate to nit pick, but why were newspapers in this area not given some notice of its arrival in local waters?'' After all, chided the paper, to the Company's increased mortification, it would only have cost the price of a stamp.

At Butedale in northern British Columbia

But the paper *did* learn of the ship's visit. The Company managed to save postage and announce the ship's arrival at the same time, simply because Captain Small, as was his custom, fired the ship's cannons as she approached the dock.

The *Nonsuch* was left to her own devices during most of the summer, making whatever stops Captain Small considered appropriate. She reached the northern boundary of her tour on June 9 when she docked at the aluminum town of Kitimat, concluding the

102

The ship's 1972 crew, from left to right:
Jan Pearce,
Richard Quinn,
John Janus,
Philip Rose-Taylor,
Tom Stevens
Jim Meckley
Sam Richards,
Alfred Weatherill
Adrian Small

longest passage of her career. The 567-mile course, which commenced in Victoria, was covered in twelve days. The weather was wet and miserable much of the time, but there were redeeming features, such as the spectacular scenery and seafood so abundant that the crew became accustomed to eating only the best fish within an hour or two of its capture. They paid a memorable visit to remote Butedale, an abandoned fish-canning centre, still completely equipped and boasting a total population of three. Captain and crew alike delighted in the excitement of sailing in historic waters travelled by Captain George Vancouver centuries before, using copies of some of Vancouver's charts which had been given to Captain Small by the British Columbia Provincial Museum in Victoria.

The *Nonsuch* did not return to the southern part of the province by the same route; instead, she followed the western coastline of Vancouver Island thus circumnavigating it or, in sailor's jargon, "viewing the island from all points of the compass." By June 19, she was within ten miles of completing her 1,127-mile round-trip course from Victoria to Kitimat, and was in the relatively familiar waters of the Strait of Juan de Fuca south-west of the British Columbia capital. She was travelling in dense fog. The Captain could not plot her position by observing visible objects like land or stars, so by calculation he estimated that the ship's position should be 4½ miles south south-east of Race Rocks. One hour later, the *Nonsuch* met the *Heather Isle,* a fishing vessel out of New Westminster, and that morning Captain Small wrote in the Log, "Only by the Grace of God did we come upon the *Heather Isle* in the fog and avoid piling up on the coast. In another five minutes, the *Nonsuch* would have been on the Rocks."

The *Nonsuch* was obligated to be in Kitimat from June 9 to 12, and was scheduled to make her grand entrance into Vancouver ten days later with the Hudson's Bay Company's Directors on board. She was to collect them at a specified point on Vancouver's North Shore and sail them across Burrard Inlet to the Kitsilano Coast-Guard Dock where she was to arrive at 8:30 p.m. Second only to Victoria, it would be the most important arrival of the season.

Although he had been bound by strict timetables in previous seasons, Captain Small still found such restrictions frustrating, and he deeply regretted that the passage to Kitimat had to be curtailled "for the sake of giving a party of Directors a trip." But despite his written displeasure concerning the cruise, his actions contradicted his words. Unimpressed with the rendezvous point selected by the Company, he set out at daybreak earlier in the week of the cruise, and guided the *Nonsuch,* as discreetly as possible, up and down the North Shore from Dunderave Pier to Lighthouse Park in search of a more pleasing alternative. He found it in Caulfield Cove, a small, thickly-wooded basin in West Vancouver which appeared to be surrounded by virgin forest, but was in fact dotted with fashionable homes. It was a splendid place to have the Directors join the ship.

Refreshments and precautionary rain-gear for all the guests were ordered and sent to the ship. Senior management personnel

The Company Directors
on board the *Nonsuch*,
bound for Vancouver;
left to right:
H. W. Sutherland,
J. B. Morgan (at the helm),
J. R. Murray,
G. R. Hunter, Q.C.,
D. S. McGiverin,
T. N. Beaupre,
A. M. McGavin,
Governor George T. Richardson

were assigned to drive the Directors to the cove, following spe-
cially-prepared maps to minimize the chance of getting lost in the
West Vancouver woods. Several yacht clubs in Greater Vancouver
had been contacted and encouraged to escort the *Nonsuch* as she
crossed Burrard Inlet; the press had been notified. The ship, of
course, was scrubbed from bow to stern.

But on June 22 it looked as if the cruise and the colourful arrival
were seriously jeopardized, for a grey, overcast sky dropped a
penetrating drizzle on Vancouver all through the day. The Directors
however, arrived at the *Nonsuch* ahead of departure time.
Undaunted and in good spirits, they climbed into the rain-gear, and

the *Nonsuch* left the charming seclusion of Caulfield Cove and motored into Burrard's calm waters.

The sailing conditions were abysmal. There was not a breath of wind, and Burrard Inlet looked as if it had been evacuated. The Company had hoped to give the Directors a taste of the ship under full sail and the festive impact of an official arrival. A rain-soaked motorcruise missed the mark altogether. Some sails were set for show, but as one was being unfurled, the water it held nearly drenched a distinguished guest below.   The liveliest activity during the first hour of the cruise was eating the boxed lunches. After that there was nothing to do, or to watch on board, for the crew were idle. Conversation became stilted. The Captain did his yeoman best to keep his guests amused by firing periodic salvos to the surprise of the people on shore, having his guests play helmsman, explaining the mysteries of the traverse board and regaling them with a judicious selection of the ship's adventures.

The lifeless *Nonsuch* plodded on. Shortly before eight o'clock, just as she reached the north-western tip of Stanley Park, the rain ceased. Almost immediately there was a break in the clouds; a gloriously warm evening sun shone through; then a sustained favourable wind sprang up. What magic! Mr. Murray, the managing director, was speechless. He had known of the ship's extraordinary good fortune, but now as he witnessed it personally, he began to believe that either God was on the Company payroll, or Poseidon was a member of the crew.

The crew scurried to carry out the commands from the helm. All sails were quickly set, and the *Nonsuch* came to life, heeling gently as she clipped along toward the Kitsilano shore in the company of several yachts which had suddenly appeared! She completed the cruise in style, announcing her arrival with eighteen salutes from her cannon, thrilling the hundreds of people who were on the dock to greet her.

Not all the ship's activities were public performances. Her visit to Dock Island to recreate "how a sailing ship was hauled out before

106

Wednesday 6th Sept. cont. ~ at Dock Island B.C.

0.00 | Ship takes the ground forward and settling steadily as tide recedes. Decks clear & night watches set.
Sam Richards on watch. Wind dropping. O'east. Baro. 1039.

W. at 35 6.8ft. | Richard Quinn on watch to 22.00. Calm. Ship firmly aground & listed against the rock wall on one upright log.
Alfred Weathwill on watch to 2300. Then Tom Stevens takes over. And so ends this day.

Light Tower.

Main yard Cock-billed

Rock wall.

upright logs.

AS.

Rocky floor.

The Nonsuch hauled out at Dock Island to scrub & paint the bottom.

A page from the Log with Captain Small's sketch of the *Nonsuch* at Dock Island

the days when docks were constructed'' went almost without notice. Dock Island, off Vancouver Island at Sidney, is really two small islets close together and covered with scrub oak. Below the northern islet, which boasts a light tower, there is a natural cutting shaped like a man-made dock. It is doubtful whether the island was ever used as a dock – the British Columbia Provincial Museum in Victoria has no record of it – but the *Nonsuch* and her crew established that it could have been.

Between September 5 and 8, Captain Small beached the *Nonsuch* at Dock Island. She was placed in the cutting bow first, with the starboard side, which rested against upright logs, fastened to the light tower and to a boulder. At low tide, the crew proceeded to scrub and paint the bottom of the forward half of the ship, either standing in the cold water or working from a raft made by Jan Pearce (recently appointed ship's mate), but always racing to complete their task before the tide came in. They also gave the wales a coat of black. The original plan was to refloat the ship and place her back in the cutting stern first in order to complete the other half, but strong winds and currents made it impossible

Well-scrubbed and almost entirely repainted below the water-line, the *Nonsuch* left Dock Island and returned to Puget Sound to resume her tour. Her season had been extended to include most of September, a proposal joyfully endorsed by the crew, a model of *esprit de corps,* who were finding the ship's climactic summer exhilarating. There was a genuine reluctance to finish the season on their part, and perhaps on the part of the ship herself, for like the stricken singer in an opera's deathbed scene, repeatedly rallying for another chorus before succumbiing to the inevitable, the *Nonsuch* continued to conclude her summer.

September 24, the end of the ship's return visit to Shilshole Bay, was the last day she was open to the public. ''The ship is closed and our tour of 1972 ended,'' noted Captain Small in the Log, and added, ''Strike the colours.'' This customary sundown ceremony was performed with dramatic flourish, but its poignancy was premature, for the next day the ship engaged in some ''fine &

pleasant sailing . . . '' with ''decks uncluttered with passengers'' in Elliott Bay off downtown Seattle. ''People in the waterside hotels & restaurants wave their napkins at us,'' wrote Captain Small. ''Do they know it is the last passage of the *Nonsuch?*''

They did not – and it was not. She spent that evening in the Duwamish River near the spot where she had been launched the previous November, and the next morning sailed north-west across Puget Sound to Kingston, where in the shallows of Appletree Cove, she grounded at the astonishing angle of 32 degrees to port. Said Captain Small ''Today's escapade makes one think the *Nonsuch* is not a little unwilling to complete this last passage.'' At high tide the ship floated free, and the Captain took her to Port Blakely where she anchored overnight.

Aground in Appletree Cove off Kingston, Washington

109

Thursday, September 28, the last day, dawned dull and over-cast, symbolic perhaps of the end which could no longer be avoided. The fresh breeze from the south, however, could not be resisted either, and Captain Small undertook a final, although brief, cruise across the Sound, through Shilshole Bay Marina where the *Nonsuch* fired her last gun, to the Seattle Shipbuilding Company yard on Lake Union. With its weathered grey buildings and dock, disused for a number of years, the yard was a dismal, and depressing place. Its channel was clogged with a rotting collection of disabled boats which blocked the entrance and had to be removed by the *Nonsuch* crew in order to get the ketch to her berth. Aesthetics, however, were of low priority. It had been important to find a quiet, secure berth adjacent to a large storage shed, and by those standards, Seattle Shipbuilding was first class – in a class by itself, in fact, for similar facilities could not be found elsewhere in Seattle.

It was suggested many times to the Company in 1972 that the *Nonsuch* operate on the West Coast for another season. This unsolicited enthusiasm for the ship came from Company employees, mayors, harbour-masters and the ordinary citizens of British Columbia and Washington who (quite understandably because of their maritime locale) were disturbed by the thought of such a fine ship being placed in a museum, and an inland one at that. Because of this response and the negligible progress on the *Nonsuch* museum in Winnipeg, the Company made sincere attempts to keep her afloat by operating her in partnership with someone else, as the Company was unwilling to continue to absorb the full costs of its popular luxury.

The *Nonsuch* was first offered to the Province of British Columbia as a tourist attraction in the province and a promotional tool for British Columbia in Puget Sound. In return for payment of the ship's operating expenses from May to September, 1973, the Company was agreeable to leasing the vessel to the Province for that period. The Washington State Historical Society, some of whose members had cruised on the ship while she was in Tacoma, was approached with similar terms, and Company executives made some personal joint-venture inquiries as well. Lastly, the Company wrote the prestigious National Geographic Society in Washington, D.C., as there was reason to believe the Society might be interested in co-sponsoring the ship as she would make an interesting feature in its magazine. All attempts to find a partner were unsuccessful.

When the *Nonsuch* eventually arrived at her winter berth at the Seattle Shipbuilding Company yard on September 28, she had travelled 2,670 miles since her April 17 shakedown cruise. Colours were struck for the last time on September 29. The voyage of the *Nonsuch* was over.

On February 9, 1973, the Hudson's Bay Company in Winnipeg received a startling telephone call from a bewildered customs broker in Sweetgrass, Montana. He managed to tell them that a truckload of *Nonsuch* parts bound for Winnipeg from Seattle had been seized by United States Customs officers, who had also forbidden further work on the *Nonsuch* in the Marco yard. The Company officials were mystified, but over the next few weeks pieces of the bizarre situation fell into place.

Seattle to Winnipeg

Unknown to the Company, when the *Nonsuch* had entered the U.S. at Sweetgrass on October 28, 1971, the customs officer on duty had instructed the Riverton men to obtain an "in transit bond," which obliged the Company to export the ship sixty days after bringing her into the country. Riverton did not inform the Company of the bond and its terms, if indeed they knew of the conditions at all.

It was not an appropriate customs entry. The Company planned to have the ship come to Seattle, be assembled in a local shipyard, exhibited and sailed on Puget Sound, travel to Canada, return to Seattle, be dismantled and shipped to Winnipeg. Not even a fraction of this could be accomplished within sixty days! If the Hudson's Bay Company had contacted U.S. Customs prior to the arrival of the vessel to advise them of its plans for her, or if the customs officer at Sweetgrass had made an effort to determine the intended use of the ship, a proper customs entry could have been made.

The entry papers that were prepared, however, were deposited with U.S. Customs in Seattle by the Riverton driver as he had been instructed to do. And then for some inexplicable reason, Customs in Seattle sat on the matter for over a year after the sixty-day period ended. Then, as if to make up for their inertia and bring the matter to a dramatic conclusion, they organized the siege at Sweetgrass on February 9, 1973, and for the first time the Company learned of the problem that had been fermenting for nearly fourteen months. By sundown that day, the Company had negotiated the release of the parts by offering the ship's hull as suitable collateral until the matter was settled.

But there was still much more to resolve. Not only had the

Nonsuch figuratively run the border, but in the eyes of the U.S. Customs, she had also blatantly contravened the Jones Act which states that "no foreign vessel shall transport passengers between ports or places in the United States, either directly or by way of a foreign port, under penalty of $200 for each passenger so transported." It was irrelevant that passengers were carried without fare and that they were usually returned to the place where they had boarded; therefore the law had been violated every time the vessel blithely carried her happy passengers in the United States.

The Hudson's Bay Company took neither the customs violation nor the siege too seriously; it found the entire situation preposterous. Company executives jokingly speculated about an equally absurd conclusion to the affair, involving Britain (the country of the ship's registry), the British Navy (on guard to aid sister ships in distress), and the Canadian Government (which might be persuaded by the Company to intervene on its behalf) – all ready to do battle with the Americans to free the hapless *Nonsuch*. This high farce had all the ingredients of another "Pig War."

U.S. Customs, on the other hand, treated these improprieties as though they were a distinct threat to the security of their country and the welfare of its people. At a meeting held in Seattle in March 1973 between Company representatives and Customs officials, a deadly earnest Customs officer sternly admonished the humbled Hudson's Bay Company for the cavalier way in which it had brought the *Nonsuch* into the States. They had some harsh (and groundless) comments about the Captain as well, concerning the way in which he had kept records of the ship's movements. No mention was made of the contribution to the problem made by their bureaucratic bungling. Seattle Customs officials refused even to discuss the matter with the Company's customs broker in Seattle and would not – or could not – answer many of his questions. By placing the blame squarely at the feet of the Company, the American Customs officers gained considerable personal relief, for they were mortified by the fiasco of the bond. They wanted the matter settled as quickly and quietly as possible.

114

From Seattle, word reached the Company that it might be penalized for its Customs violation, and a fine in the neighbourhood of $245,000 was mentioned, the amount U.S. Customs believed to be the value of the ship. They did not impose the penalty, but in return Customs insisted that the Company export every piece of *Nonsuch* it had brought into the country in 1971. The Company had not planned to do this. Upon the ship's return to Seattle the previous September, Captain Small had sold the ship's life-preservers to another vessel. In the course of the winter the Company had found prospective buyers in Seattle for all the ship's modern equipment, which was not required in Winnipeg to display the *Nonsuch* as a period piece. Not wanting to embarrass or irritate U.S. Customs further, the Company agreed, and two shipments of *Nonsuch* goods were loaded to be sent to Vancouver under the casual supervision of two novice Customs officials who had never heard of the *Nonsuch*. One shipment consisted of the lead ballast and keel; the other included such varied articles as the ship's engine, water tanks, eight feet of rubber hose and two well-worn scrubbing brushes.

The Company decided to wait until September to bring the rest of the *Nonsuch* to Winnipeg. The weather would still be favourable then, and the peak summer tourist traffiic would have returned home from holidays. U.S. Customs agreed to this, provided that the ship was protected. She was perfectly safe in the Marco yard, parked on her side in her cradle immediately outside the firm's administrative offices, and throughout the summer, arrangements for the return journey were made with an ease unknown in 1971.

When the day of departure arrived, the *Nonsuch* was stubbornly unco-operative about leaving her long-time Seattle home: she ran aground on an asphalt hump at the top of the inclined exit road from the yard, and could not be coaxed over it. To the inexperienced, the obstacle seemed insuperable, but to Chris Thorsteinson, Icelandic Houdini, master of the art of ship extrication, it was merely another challenge. Under his direction planks were placed under the wheels near the stern of the ship, raising her over the obstruction. It was the only problem the ship encountered on the entire journey to Winnipeg.

But although the *Nonsuch* was rolling eastward with remarkable alacrity, her Winnipeg home was in a state of extreme unreadiness.

Between 1967, when the *Nonsuch* replica was officially announced, and 1971, progress on the ship's museum home had been negligible. Sites had been considered, some preliminary architectural drawings had been prepared and some funds had been raised. But that was all. The Manitoba election of 1969 replaced the Progressive Conservative party, which had been in office when the *Nonsuch* project was announced, with the New Democrats, who were unfamiliar with the previous government's commitment to the ship. On November 22 of the following year, Maitland Steinkopf, chairman of the provincial government's Manitoba Centennial Corporation, died of a heart attack. He had been the driving administrator of both the 1967 Canadian Centennial celebrations in Manitoba and the Provincial Centennial in 1970. The building to house the *Nonsuch* was one of many centennial projects that centred around this remarkable man. Mr. Steinkopf died leaving a legacy of guesswork regarding the funds for the various projects he had promoted; he knew the sources but it was his habit to keep them to himself.

The Company began to have misgivings about the future of the *Nonsuch* building.

With the change in provincial administration, they had become concerned that the absence of a formal document might result in their gift to the Province being returned, as they had made three unsuccessful attempts to have the government sign an agreement regarding the *Nonsuch*. However, during the uncertain time at the beginning of the New Democratic era, and amid the financial confusion that followed the death of Mr. Steinkopf, there was never any indication that the government was attempting to shirk its *Nonsuch* obligation or renege because of lack of funds. Indeed, exactly a month after Mr. Steinkopf's death, his successor reassured

116

the Company that the proposed *Nonsuch* building would be realized.

In 1971 the Manitoba Centennial Corporation established a committee charged with the responsibility of building a museum, not just a boathouse for the *Nonsuch,* but a building to house a number of transportation items indigenous to Winnipeg or the Canadian West. The committee, under the chairmanship of C. Gordon Smith, pursued this multiple end until July 1972, when they were persuaded by Dr. A.E. Parr, a respected museum consultant, to devote the entire building to the *Nonsuch.*

And at last, on a warm, sunny August 22, 1973, the sod-turning ceremony for the Nonsuch Museum took place. The noon-hour affair included representatives of the Manitoba Centennial Corporation, the Hudson's Bay Company and the Manitoba Museum of Man and Nature, and a number of neighbourhood children inappropriately dressed as pirates. It was just over six years since the Company and the Province had jointly announced the reconstruction of the vessel and her permanent berth in Winnipeg.

Less than a month later, the *Nonsuch* arrived at the outskirts of Winnipeg; she had completed the journey from Seattle in only eleven days.

The ship's arrival in Winnipeg came much sooner than anticipated, well ahead of the time she was scheduled to be placed on the concrete foundation of the museum, which still had to be poured and set. Although arrangements had been made to park the *Nonsuch* overnight in the vicinity of the museum, it was obvious that she would be there much longer than that. Chris Thorsteinson had often said the ship was welcome on the Riverton Boatworks premises should the need arise, and now this seemed an excellent solution. After spending the weekend at a service station just west of Winnipeg, the *Nonsuch* was taken to the Riverton yard ninety miles north of the city, where she remained until November 19.

It is quite probable that when the original ketch reached the bleak southern shore of James Bay in late September 1668, she was

A giant crane lifts the hull into the Nonsuch Museum

118

The museum under
construction

An aerial view of the Nonsuch Museum with the hull in place

greeted by snow. Her replica arrived in Winnipeg in the midst of a modest blizzard which reduced visibility and annoyed photographers who had awaited this arrival for weeks, if not years. On the morning of November 20, the bolts securing the *Nonsuch* to the iron cradle were cut, and by sundown a giant crane had lifted the *Nonsuch* and placed her in position on the museum floor. More damage was done to the ship that day than in the five years since her launching. On the first attempted lift-off, two oak planks on the starboard side amidships were sliced like cheese by one of the lifting cables; there had been insufficient wedging between the hull and the sling. During the rest of the day, carvings were scraped, the starboard mizzen channel was fractured and a 43-inch piece of the poop railing was amputated by a cable. The *Nonsuch* was supported overnight by the iron slings, and the next day, her deck still covered with four inches of snow, she was braced upright by supports placed under the bilge.

Work on the building recommenced toward the end of the month, and by springtime the building was enclosed, entombing the *Nonsuch* forever in steel and precast concrete.

Captain Small had always had reservations about the ship's destiny. On the day of the Directors' cruise in Vancouver, he made the following entry in the Log, which he recommended that each passenger read: "A dry-land berth for the ship inside a museum building in Winnipeg, Manitoba, is a dismal prospect for a well-found, seaworthy & new vessel. Not only that but she is the *only* example of a 17 century type of vessel afloat & available for historians (& general public) to inspect in a sea-going condition."

He realized, however, that the ship's fate was sealed, and when he came to Winnipeg in October 1972, he chose to do all he could to see that his beloved ship was properly and effectively presented in the museum. At a meeting with some members of the Building Committee, he suggested the replica "be depicted as fitting out for sea – for the voyage to Canada . . . ."

"The ship is seen secured alongside a small stone quay at Deptford on the River Thames in the spring of 1668. It is low tide & the ship rests on a hard gravel sandy bed so that her underwater hull is visible. Mooring ropes secure her to the quay. The sails are loosed to dry and may be in disarray. Cannons & stores are arranged on the quay ready for loading. The shallop is alongside & the ship's gig is on the quay being repaired. The quay is fronted by a warehouse and workshops inside which are a rigging shop, a rope walk, blockmakers, coopers, sail loft with sails being made, ship-wrights constructing a small boat, a ship's chandler & office. Prince Rupert or King Charles could be visiting Captain Gillam to inspect progress. Mast-makers could be shaping up a spare topmast on the quay. Ropes, blocks, wood shavings etc. would be very much in evidence. Two shipwrights could be caulking the hull near the rudder."

The people in the meeting were captivated by Adrian Small's imaginative proposal; no one else had thought of making the setting and the ship complementary to one another. It gave life to what could have been a static display, and continued the ideal of authenticity which the Company had stressed in the construction of

Epilogue

In the Nonsuch Museum

the replica. The concept was unanimously endorsed by the Building Committee.

In the middle of May 1974, about a month before the museum commenced construction of the dockside scene, the Hudson's Bay Company assembled Captain Small, Jan Pearce, Sam Richards and Dick Barnett (a shipwright from the Hinks yard) to lead a team of paid and volunteer help to refit the *Nonsuch* in Winnipeg. This would be the Company's final obligation to the ship that had brought it so much glory, for on January 31, 1974, she had become museum property.

The refit in Winnipeg was unlike any other in the ship's life, in that it was carried out indoors without interference from the weather. But the *Nonsuch* was a sorry sight and had more than her usual voracious appetite for labour. In addition to the arduous tasks of stepping masts, hoisting yards and bending sail, the men had to catch up on two years' maintenance work, for the ship had not been touched since returning to Seattle in the fall of 1972. Cracks had opened her parched wood. Oakum hung from her widened seams like unmanageable hair. About a hundred bolt holes scarred her starboard side and had to be plugged. An advanced case of rot had to be cut out of an eight-foot section of the main lowermast. The maintop had rotted so badly, it required rebuilding entirely.

Today, some of her scars, nicks, and worn spots remain, cherished symbols of her colourful days as a sailing ship. These blemishes were important to Adrian Small. He campaigned for their retention and regretted that he had ordered the hull below the waterline to be scraped bare of barnacles acquired on the Pacific. The Company and the museum again endorsed his suggestion; everyone agreed that without these signs of life, the museum *Nonsuch* might look like a ship that had never seen the sea.

In her inland home, she remains a striking reminder of the little ship that accomplished so much centuries ago, whose tradition of adventure, good fortune and success she continued in her own contemporary way. Experts have called the *Nonsuch* the most authentic replica built by modern man; certainly she is an enduring tribute to the Hudson's Bay Company, who had the vision, the spirit and the wherewithal to have her built with such care and to sail her in four countries where thousands could share in her magic.

The *Nonsuch* against a seventeenth-century quay, as depicted by Adrian Small

125

Appendix

Form No. 9

PRESCRIBED BY THE
COMMISSIONERS OF
CUSTOMS & EXCISE
with THE CONSENT
OF
THE BOARD
OF TRADE

CERTIFICATE OF BRITISH REGISTRY

PARTICULARS OF SHIP

Official Number	Name of Ship	No., Year and Port of Registry	No., Year and Port of previous Registry (if any)
336966	Nonsuch	527 in 1968 London	

Whether a Sailing, Steam or Motor Ship; if Steam or Motor, how propelled

Sailing and Auxiliary Motor Ship Single Screw

	Where Built	When Built	Name and Address of Builders
	Appledore	1968	J. Hinks & Son, Appledore, N. Devon.

			FEET	TENTHS
Number of Decks	One	Length from fore-part of stem, to the aft side of the head of the stern post for side of the rudder stock	50	0
Number of Masts	Two	Main breadth to outside of planking plating amidships	15	4
Rigged	Ketch	Depth in hold from tonnage deck to ceiling amidships	7	6.5
Stem	Cutter	Depth in hold from upper deck to ceiling amidships, in the case of two decks and upwards		
Stern	Transom	Depth from top of upper deck at side amidships to bottom of bar keel	9	1
Build	Carvel	Round of beam on upper deck	-	5
Framework and description of vessel	Two COLOUR (Portion of Oak) One Mahogany, Half 1056)	Length of engine-room (if any)	3	6
Number of Bulkheads				

PARTICULARS OF PROPELLING ENGINES, &c. (IF ANY), as supplied by Builders, Owners, or Engine Makers.

	When made	Name and Address of Makers
Engines	1968	Perkins Engines Ltd., Peterborough.
Boilers		

Particulars of Boilers

Description ..

Number ..

	Description of Engines		Reciprocating Engines			Rotary Engines	N.H.P. B.H.P. I.H.P. Estimated Speed of Ship
			No. of cylinders in each set	Diameter of cylinders		No. of cylinders in each set	
No. of sets of Engines	Internal Combustion Four Stroke Cycle Single Acting		Six	3.6"			64 at 2000 r.p.m.
One							
No. of Shafts				Length of Stroke			~
One				5"			8 knots

The tonnages of this ship in accordance with her British Tonnage Certificate are :—

GROSS TONNAGE   37.64   tons (106.52   cubic metres)

REGISTER TONNAGE   37.25   tons (105.42   cubic metres)

Delete if not applicable

This ship is assigned with a tonnage mark on each side of the ship which is ....inches below the upper deck line and when this mark is submerged the above tonnages are applicable.

When the tonnage mark is **NOT** submerged the following tonnages are applicable :—

GROSS TONNAGE ....tons (...................cubic metres)

REGISTER TONNAGE ....tons (...................cubic metres)

A detailed summary of the tonnages for this ship is shown on The British Tonnage Certificate.

The number of seamen and apprentices for whom accommodation is certified ......*Nil.*......

I, the undersigned, Registrar of British Ships at the Port of ......*London*......, hereby certify that the Ship, the Description of which is prefixed to this my Certificate, has been duly surveyed, and that the above Description is in accordance with the Register Book ; that *Adrian Victor Orford Small,* whose Certificate of Competency or Service is No. *76887*......, is the Master of the said Ship ; and that the Name......, Residence and Description of the Owner ......, and Number of Sixty-fourth Shares held by *it*......, are as follows :—

Name, Residence, and Occupation of the Owner.	Number of Sixty-fourth Shares.
The Governor and Company of Adventurers of England trading into Hudson's Bay (Hudson's Bay Company) having its principal place of business at Beaver House, Great Trinity Lane, E.C.4, in the City of London.	Sixty-four

Dated at *H.M. Custom House, London,* the *16th* day of *December,* One thousand nine hundred *and sixty-eight.*

Barwell.

Registrar of British Ships.

NOTICE.—A Certificate of Registry is not a document of Title. It does not necessarily contain notice of all changes of ownership, and in no case does it contain an official record of any mortgages affecting the ship. In case of any change of ownership it is important for the protection of the interests of all parties that the change should be registered according to law. Changes of ownership, address or other registered particulars should be notified to the Registrar at the Port of Registry. Should the Vessel be lost, sold to Foreigners, or broken up, notice thereof, together with the Certificate of Registry, if in existence, should immediately be given to the Registrar of British Ships at the Port of Registry under a Penalty of £100 for default.

Instruction to Registrars of British Ships, paragraphs 182-185   Sec. F.3081 (Jan. 1967).

C. 344C.

8604 (76613B) 22186 10m (P) 12/66 S(P&D)L

This vessel, a replica of the seventeenth-century ketch *Nonsuch* believed to have been built in 1650, was built at Appledore, Devon, by J. Hinks & Son and launched in August 1968. The hull is constructed of oak.

Basic Characteristics

Port of Registry – London, England
Official Number – 336966
Gross tons – 37.64
Register tons – 37.25
Displacement (at normal draught) – 75 tons
Sailing draught forward – 9 feet
Sailing draught aft – 9 feet 10 inches
Minimum freeboard – 2 feet
Registered dimensions – 50 feet x 15.4 feet x 7.7 feet
Length from stem to stern – 54 feet
Length including bowsprit – 75 feet
Maximum breadth – 17 feet 9 inches
Height from bottom of keel to top of mainmast – 80 feet

Description of Rig

The *Nonsuch* carries the typical ketch rig of the seventeenth century, consisting of two square-rigged masts, the main and mizzen, and a bowsprit. All her masts and spars are Scotch pine.

The mainmast consists of three spars of the following lengths:
    Main lowermast, 45 feet
    Main topmast, 25 feet 3 inches
    Main topgallantmast, 14 feet 3 inches

The mizzenmast consists of two spars of the following lengths:
Mizzen lowermast, 37 feet
Mizzen topmast, 16 feet 6 inches

The bowsprit is one spar, 31 feet 6 inches long.

Her yards are the following lengths:
Main yard, 34 feet
Main topsail yard, 19 feet
Main topgallant yard, 12 feet
Crossjack yard, 19 feet
Mizzen topsail yard, 12 feet
Lateen yard, 28 feet
Spritsail yard, 22 feet
Ensign staff, 16 feet
Jack staff, 7 feet 6 inches

The masts are supported by hemp shrouds, stays and backstays.
The shrouds and backstays are set up with elm deadeyes and hemp
lanyards to outboard channels of oak. The main channels project 18
inches from the ship's sides amidships, two feet above the waterline.
Her hand-sewn flax sails are of the following approximate areas:
Jib, 141$\frac{3}{4}$ square feet
Jib bonnet, 81$\frac{1}{4}$ square feet
Staysail, 114 square feet
Staysail bonnet, 82$\frac{1}{2}$ square feet
Mainsail, 525 square feet
Main bonnet, 195 square feet
Main topsail, 439 square feet
Main topgallantsail, 56$\frac{1}{2}$ square feet
Lateen mizzen, 132 square feet
Mizzen bonnet, 67 square feet
Mizzen topsail, 123 square feet
Spritsail, 190 square feet
Total sail area, 2,147 square feet